PENGUIN BOOKS

DEAR MISTER ROGERS

Fred Rogers, creator of the daily PBS children's program, *Mister Rogers' Neighborhood,* is also founder and chairman of Family Communications, Inc., a nonprofit company dedicated to producing materials in all media for children, their families, and those who support them. His home is in Pittsburgh, Pennsylvania.

Dear Mister Rogers,

Does it ever rain in your Neighborhood?

Letters to Mister Rogers

FRED ROGERS

PENGUIN BOOKS

PENGUIN BOOKS
Published by the Penguin Group
Penguin Books USA Inc., 375 Hudson Street,
New York, New York 10014, U.S.A.
Penguin Books Ltd, 27 Wrights Lane, London W8 5TZ, England
Penguin Books Australia Ltd, Ringwood, Victoria, Australia
Penguin Books Canada Ltd, 10 Alcorn Avenue,
Toronto, Ontario, Canada M4V 3B2
Penguin Books (N.Z.) Ltd, 182–190 Wairau Road, Auckland 10, New Zealand

Penguin Books Ltd, Registered Offices: Harmondsworth, Middlesex, England

First published in Penguin Books 1996

10 9 8 7 6 5 4 3 2 1

Portions of this work appeared in Fred Rogers's *Mister Rogers Talks with
Parents* (Hal Leonard Corporation) and his newspaper column, "Insights into
Childhood" (King Features Syndicate).

The song lyrics in this book are reprinted from the following compositions:
"Good People Sometimes Do Bad Things," © 1972, Fred M. Rogers; "It's the
People You Like the Most," © 1972, Fred M. Rogers; "Some Things I Don't
Understand," © 1971, Fred M. Rogers; "Sometimes People Are Good," ©
1967, Fred M. Rogers; "What Do You Do?," © 1968, Fred M. Rogers;
"Wishes Don't Make Things Come True," © 1970, Fred M. Rogers.

Library of Congress Cataloging in Publication Data
Rogers, Fred.
    Dear Mister Rogers: does it ever rain in your neighborhood?/
Fred Rogers.
      p. cm.
   ISBN 0 14 02.3515 9 (pbk.)
    1. Rogers, Fred—Correspondence.   2. Mister Rogers' neighborhood
(Television program)   I. Title.
PN1992.4.R56A4   1996
791.45'028'092—dc20   [B]   95-47936

Printed in the United States of America
Set in Minion

To anyone who has ever cared to write a "Dear Mister Rogers" letter:

With gratitude for your loving trust.

Acknowledgments

Extra special thanks go to all the people who have ever written to our Neighborhood—people who have shared with us what is important in their lives. We have treasured everything—published or not—that has come to us from our television friends.

Through the years, as we worked hard to give a meaningful answer to a letter, we felt blessed to have the wisdom and understanding of our longtime consultants, Dr. Margaret McFarland and Dr. Albert Corrado. They and others have helped us find ways to be personal and sensitive and yet recognize the limits of trying to know someone only through a letter.

For over twenty-five years, Hedda Sharapan, along with her many other responsibilities at Family Communications, has been the Neighborhood's chief mail person. It's only because of Hedda's understanding, dedication, and enthusiasm for our treasure of letters and drawings that this book could become a reality.

Special thanks to Marcy Wade and Elaine Lynch, who have worked at proofreading, typing, gathering enclosures, and all the other administrative effort that it takes to get our responses into the mail. It has always meant a great deal to me to know that they have handled this work with real care and appreciation for the people who receive the letters from us.

Thanks also to the interns and volunteers who, over the past twenty-five years, have filed the letters once they were answered, so that we could find them easily. One intern who deserves recognition for her work on this particular book is Heather Arnet. Through her persistent searching, she found many of the families whose letters and pictures we wanted to share in this book.

As always, our thanks to our editor at Viking, Mindy Werner, and our friend and colleague, Dennis Ciccone, who gave us fresh perspectives and continual encouragement for putting our letters into a form that others could enjoy.

I'm always grateful to my teachers, my friends, and my family: Joanne, Jim and Tory, Alexander and Douglas, John and Mary, and everyone who has been a part of our television Neighborhood. All these years of corresponding with children and their families have been gifts which know no measure.

Contents

CONTENTS

Introduction

Dear Reader,

"Won't You Be My Neighbor?" I've always thought of that opening song of ours as an invitation. It's an invitation to be close. To share thoughts and feelings. To talk about things that matter to us.

But when I'm making our program in the television studio, I can't know each person who's responding to the invitation to be my "television neighbor." That's probably why I've come to treasure the mail so much. "Dear Mister Rogers," to me, is a way people have of saying, "Yes, I will be your neighbor . . . and here's something I'd like to tell you that matters to me."

Just as our program is a "television visit," the mail is a "letter visit." It gives me a way to know my neighbors as real people and to make a more personal connection with them.

In fact, that connection has always been an important part of my work. I can remember sitting around the dining room table with my wife and answering by hand all of the mail that came from the children and families who watched *Misterogers*, the forerunner of *Mister Rogers' Neighborhood*, which we produced in Toronto at the CBC (Canadian Broadcasting Corporation) in the early 1960s. Our table would be piled high with letters and drawings, and as soon as we had our boys in their beds, we would work until late at night, answering every one.

Even now, one of the first things I do each day when I come to the office is to work on the letters that have arrived from the children and adults who have written to us. I still care deeply about sending a personal response. Because we receive almost four thousand letters a year, and because we continue our work on our Neighborhood program and other projects, there are often delays in answering; nevertheless, we still want to give attention to each one.

Of course, sometimes letters have no return addresses, so there's no way we can respond. But we try as best we can with the resources that we have, and we hope that people understand.

What's changed in the mail over the years? Looking back, it seems that what children or adults write about hasn't changed all that much.

Lately, though, at least once a day, we hear from teenagers and young adults who tell us that even now they stop and look at our program and want us to know how much our

Neighborhood visits meant to them as they were growing up. Some young adults already have children of their own or are working with young children, and they tell me what it means to them to be able to share the Neighborhood experience with the next generation.

The real challenge in answering the letters that come to me is that I can know the letter writer only from what he or she has written. As you might imagine, many people tell personal stories and describe deep feelings. I've always tried to respond in a way that respects whatever that person may be feeling. At the same time, I've been careful not to answer as a "therapist." While I've studied extensively in child development, I can be only a television friend to those who watch and write. That's different from being a real friend. I've tried to make that clear over the years on our program, as well as in the mail. I firmly believe that the most meaningful help comes from someone who can know us in a real and ongoing way, and I've encouraged people who write to me asking for advice or people who seem troubled to do all they can to find a flesh-and-blood kind of supportive relationship in their families, schools, or spiritual, mental health, or medical communities.

Over the years, we've received many treasures in the mail! We've saved all those letters and stored them carefully and caringly. As you can imagine, the hardest part of developing this book was choosing which letters and pictures to include.

Besides that, we contacted each letter writer for his or her permission. There were a number of disappointing days here in our office when those letters came back unopened, with a notice from the post office saying that the addressee had moved and couldn't be traced.

But, happily, there were many who did receive the letter and even responded with updates about families since the last time we were in touch. Many wrote proudly about how much they've grown and changed. One family who had written to tell us about a miscarriage several years ago now gave us the exciting news that there was a new baby in their home. A mother who had written about her son's unwillingness to wear his eye patch said she had found more medical opinions and finally came upon a pediatric ophthalmologist who helped their family enormously. She added, "I'm no longer afraid to speak up."

One boy told us, "I was glad you wrote back to me the first time because it made me sure that you were real. But how could you not be real? Would they just use one big model for you? Or a robot? Or did they do that a long time ago, did I think it was far away and a long time ago when you were alive and you didn't exist anymore?"

One family told us they kept our response in their son's scrapbook and "love to look at it, read it, and remember how little he was and how far we've come."

As you read through this book, you may be inspired to have a "letter visit" with someone *you* care about. Sharing some of your thoughts and feelings, letting him or her know what matters to you right now: that would be one of the best outcomes a book like this could have.

We human beings want to be reminded that we're not alone—that people care about us, even when we're not near. However we may help to do that is—in my mind—being a welcome "neighbor."

Sincerely,

Fred Rogers

P.S. In putting this book together, we included not only excerpts from letters from our viewers, but also parts of our answers, because we thought you might like to see them. Here and there, I've also included some of my personal thoughts about the letters. If these reflections prompt you to think about things in your own life and relationships with the children who are important to you, the publication of this book will be well worth the work, the ink, and the paper.

Dear Mister Rogers

CHAPTER ONE

Are you real?

(Emma, age 5)

Dear Mister Rogers,

Are you for real? Are you under a mask or costume like Big Bird? Are you for real? Are you for real or not? My birthday wish is I want to know if you are for real.

Timmy, age 5

Dear Timmy,

. . . That's a good question. It's hard for children to understand what they see on television. I'm glad that you are a person who wonders about things and that you ask questions about what you're wondering. Asking questions is a good way to grow and learn!

You asked if I am a real person. I am a real person, just the way you are a real person. There are some things on television that aren't real—the cartoons and the monsters and scary things like that, but I'm a real person. Your television set is a special way that you can see the picture of me and hear my voice. I can't look out through the television set to see or hear my television friends, but I think about them whenever we make our television visits.

Dear Mister Rogers,
Do you live in there?
            Philip, age 4½

❀ That letter reminded me of a time a young boy came up to me and said in amazement, "Mister Rogers! How did you get out of the box!"

We've heard about children who have walked around behind the television trying to see how the people get in and out of there. A child I know waited excitedly at the heels of the television repairman for the moment when the back panel would be removed to reveal what he thought would surely be a little world with tiny people inside.

Another young man told us that when he was a boy, he would run around to the back of his television when our program was over, cupping his hands under the set, hoping to catch me as I came out!

Dear Mister Rogers,
Sometimes I get nervous when Purple Panda & Bob Dog
come too close to the t.v.

Emily, age 4

Dear Emily,
. . . I understand that some things on television can be
scary for children, and I'm glad you can talk about
what is upsetting for you.

Some children might worry that if scary things
come too close to the camera, those things might get
out of the television. I know it's hard to understand
how television works, but, Emily, the things you see on
television can't get out. I am not inside your television,
and the people in the Bob Dog and Purple Panda
costumes on our program aren't inside the television
either; a television set is just a way that a picture can
be shown in people's homes. It can take a long while
to understand about television, and I'm glad you
wanted to share your feelings about Purple Panda and
Bob Dog with me.

Dear Mister Rogers,
When I talk to you, you don't listen. Also, I wanted to
know, are you real in real life?

Colin, age 4½

Dear Mister Rogers,
Do you know me?
Gordon, age 4

Dear Neighbor,
. . . I know it can be hard to understand about
television. . . . I can't look out through the television
set to see or hear my television friends when we make
our program, and that's why I'm especially glad when
they want to write to me so that I can get to know
them as real people. I was pleased to know you from
your letter.

❊ One of our favorite letters came from a very sensitive and
loving father describing a conversation he had with his three-
and-a-half-year-old son, Isaac, who had been struggling with
the question about how real I was.

Dear Mister Rogers,
While putting [my son] to bed last night, he said, "Mr.
Rogers doesn't poop [i.e., defecate]." I said that of course
you did. He denied it vehemently. I asked where his
certainty came from and he said, "Well, I've never seen
him poop." I pointed out that there were lots of people
he hadn't seen poop, and they all still did. He accepted
that about others [adults and kids], but denied it about
you. I kissed him goodnight and left the room. Five
minutes later I was summoned to his bedside. "Daddy, I
know Mr. Rogers doesn't poop." "How?" I asked.
"Because I've seen his house, and he just has a closet, a
living room, a kitchen, and a yard."

Sincerely,
Isaac's father

Dear Isaac,

. . . Your father told me you had an interesting talk
with him about whether I "poop." It's good that you
and he were talking about that. I know it can be hard
to understand that I do. I am a real person. And, one
thing for certain is that all real people "poop." That is
an important part of how our bodies work. Little by
little as you grow, you will learn more about how our

bodies work. And it is good that you are thinking about that now.

On some of our programs I show the bathroom in my television house. It is off to the side of the kitchen. . . . We don't often show the bathroom of our television set because that is not my real house. I think of it as my "television house." That is a place where I stop by during my workday to have a television visit with my friends. When I am at work, I use the bathrooms in the building where we make our programs.

❀ Here's an excerpt from the letter we sent to Isaac's father:

Dear Mr. ———,
Your letter was absolutely refreshing! . . . Thank you for all that you shared with us, especially for the conversation you had with Isaac about my bodily functions. That's such a wonderful story to attest to young children's focus on "bathroom" concerns.

But what particularly struck me was the way you were so sensitive to your son's questions and that you were willing to help him think the issues through, even with a subject that can be as sensitive as that. Your son is indeed fortunate to have a father like you.

❀ When we talk with children about television, it's just as important to listen to how children have figured out things. I've always enjoyed the way they express their ideas about the people on television:

Dear Mister Rogers,
I didn't know that you weren't only on tv. I didn't know that you lived.

Josiah, age 5

Dear Mister Rogers,
What did you think about how to get on tv? Did you just get on tv without thinking about your stuff? Or did you think about the stuff you were going to do? Did you go to a store with a little door when there was a little screen? Did you open the door and then be inside the TV by turning on the channel that showed your face? It's true that I watch you on TV, but I have to wonder how

you got on *TV because I don't know. I want to know so I could tell the secrets to the kids in my class, like Kacey, who is coming over today.*

Sarah, age 4½

Dear Mister Rogers,
I wish you accidentally stepped out of the tv into my house so that I could play with you.

Danny, age 5

Dear Mister Rogers,
I didn't know you were real until Mom told me. I thought you were a puppet. But then I saw your feet. I thought you had a hole in your back. That's because you're on TV, and people on TV are characters. But mom says you're real, too.

Tony, age 4

Dear Mister Rogers,
Sometimes when I watch television I have trouble knowing when the people are pretending. I don't know if you live in your house on television. I don't know if you are a real person on TV or if you are somebody else.

Amber, age 5

Dear Mister Rogers,
I would like to know how you get in the tv.
                    Robby, age 4

Dear Mister Rogers,
I wish you could be on Earth.
                    Nicholas, age 3

Dear Mister Rogers,
How do I see you on tv when you live in another place?
Your face can't go through the plug.
                    Shlomiya, age 6

❁ While I can give some general answers in the mail about television, what's most helpful is that children have caring adults who can be more specific and who can continue to talk with them whenever those kinds of concerns arise. So my answers usually include something like this:

Dear Neighbor,
. . . Maybe you and the grown-ups in your family could talk more about what is real and what isn't. Whenever you see something on any television

program that's confusing for you, it's good to ask. You are fortunate to have a family who cares about you and your questions.

❀ It's obvious that young children have a hard time understanding about television. They're trying to figure out how the world works, and one of their major tasks is to discover what in this world is real and what is pretend. Television can be especially confusing because it has things like special effects, animations, and close-ups that often distort the lines between reality and fantasy.

Questions like "Are you real?" also help confirm something I've long believed: children do need grown-ups nearby when they're watching television to help with their wonderings. We can't take for granted that children understand what they see and hear on television.

What do children need from adults in those kinds of discussions? For something as complicated and abstract as television, the children certainly don't need technical answers. Even simple explanations may not work. When I explained to the boy who asked "How did you get out of the box?" that television was just a way to show pictures, he nodded through the whole explanation, as if he understood. Then he asked, "But, Mister Rogers! How are you going to get back *in?!*"

Most important of all in those conversations about television is to let children know that their questions are important, that we care about whatever they're wondering. That gives them clear messages that we're proud of them for the important work they're doing of trying to make sense of the world.

What we attempt to do on *Mister Rogers' Neighborhood* is create a comfortable starting place to begin talking about what television is . . . and isn't, what's real and what isn't.

Many children have found it comforting to learn that I *am* a real person and that I live in a real house with a real family. I think that they have found it reassuring, too, to know that this real Mister Rogers is a grown-up who really does care about how children grow—and that's why he makes television programs for them.

CHAPTER TWO

Do you have a job?

(Daniel, age 5)

Dear Mister Rogers,
I don't see a mother or kids in your house. Do you have any?

Justin, age 3

Dear Justin,
. . . My mother and my father died several years ago, when I was already grown and married. I have a wife and two grown sons, James and John. Our sons are both married, and they live in their own homes with their families. My wife and I don't live at our television house. That's just the place where I make our television program. We live in a real home somewhere else in Pittsburgh.

Dear Mister Rogers,
How is your home? When do you take a shower? Where
are your children?

Brian, age 3

Dear Brian,
. . . We haven't shown my real house on our television
visits because my family and I think of that as a
private place for us. You might want to imagine what
our real home is like. You might even want to draw
some pictures about it.

Dear Mister Rogers,
Our son Alex wants to know if you ever get angry.

Alex's mom and dad

Dear Alex,
In your parents' letter, they told us that you've had
some talks about when people have angry feelings in
families. That reminds me of one of our songs, "It's
the People You Like the Most." I wonder if you know
the words:

It's the people you like the most
Who can make you feel maddest.
It's the people you care for the most
Who manage to make you feel baddest.

It's the people you like the most
Who can make you feel happiest!
It's the people you care for the most, most likely,
Who manage to make you feel snappiest!

You wondered if I ever get angry. Of course I do;
everybody gets angry sometimes. But, Alex, each
person has his and her way of showing angry feelings.
Usually, if I'm angry, I play loud and angry sounds on
the piano. Or, sometimes I swim very fast, and that
helps me with my mad feelings. I think that finding
ways of showing our feelings—ways that don't hurt
ourselves or anybody else—is one of the most
important things we can learn to do.

What helps you when you're angry? It's good that
you and your parents talk about things like that. I
have always called talking about feelings "important
talk." You are fortunate to have a mother and father
who care so much about you and about your feelings.

Dear Mister Rogers,
Were you ever naughty?
> *William, age 2*

Dear Mister Rogers,
Did you get in trouble when you were little?
> *Becky, age 7, and Danny, age 4*

Dear Neighbor,

I think everyone sometimes does things that are upsetting to other people. When I was a boy, I didn't like it when I did something like that, but it did happen once in a while.

We have a Neighborhood song about times like that . . . "Good People Sometimes Do Bad Things." We are sending you the words to that song, but you might like to make up your own songs about good people and bad things.

GOOD PEOPLE SOMETIMES DO BAD THINGS

Good people sometimes think bad things,
Good people dream bad things, don't you?
Good people even say bad things,
Once in a while we do.

Good people sometimes wish bad things,
Good people try bad things, don't you?
Good people even do bad things,
Once in a while we do.

Has anybody said you're good lately?
Has anybody said you're nice?
And have you wondered how they could, lately,
Wondered once or twice?

Did you forget that
Good people sometimes feel bad things?
Good people want bad things, they do!
Good people even do bad things
Once in a while we do,
Good people sometimes do.

Dear Mister Rogers,
Can I please be with you in your house? I want to visit
you. I'm good at thinking, coloring, singing, dancing,
eating, and loving.

Charlie, age 4

Dear Charlie,

It meant a lot to me to know you'd like to have a real visit with us. I am sorry that is not possible. We don't usually have children on our program because I like to think of that time as a "television visit" with the children who are watching television. And, we can't invite our friends here because there is no area for guests in the studio where we make our television program. Even though we can't have a real visit, it is good that we can have television visits whenever you're watching. And, you might want to make up your own stories about a visit we could have. For your pretending, things can be any way you want them to be.

Because we aren't able to have a real visit, I enjoy getting to know my television friends through the mail. I was glad to know some important things about you, that you're good at thinking, coloring, singing, dancing, eating, and loving. I'm proud to have a television friend like you.

Dear Mister Rogers,
My Daddy works at Sears. Do you have a job, too?
                                        Steven, age 7

Dear Steven,
. . . It was good to know about your father's work. My job is making our television visits, and I'm glad to know I have a television friend like you who is watching.

❀ Sometimes children have asked what I do at my work, and I tell them that there's a lot of planning that goes into making a television program. Part of my work is thinking of the ideas for our television visits and writing the scripts and songs. Then we have a lot of meetings so that everything will be ready for us when we go into the studio to make our program. Another important part of my work is answering the mail from my television friends.

Dear Mister Rogers,
*   Hello. I'm a freshman in high school. For my English class, I must write a letter to someone in the public eye and ask them what their "great expectations" were in high school.*

My first question is who did you want to be when you grew up? What did you want to spend the rest of your life doing? Did you live up to your own expectations?

My great expectations are to be a writer or to help girls who are [in trouble] or just to be someone who cares for them. I want to be a writer so that I can expand my mind.

Courtney, age 14

Dear Courtney,

. . . You asked about my expectations when I was growing up, and I'm glad to share some of those with you in this letter. When I was a teenager, my expectation was that I would be a songwriter. Music was a big part of my life throughout my childhood and teenage years. I never expected to be on television. There wasn't such a thing as television when I was a boy. But I do compose the songs for our program, so in a way, I am fulfilling that expectation. I think what helped me was hard work and the grace of God. Like the main character in the book *Great Expectations*, I was fortunate to have many people who helped me learn and grow along the way.

You're such a warm and expressive writer, Courtney, and that is a wonderful gift for you to bring to whatever you do in the future, whether it's through writing or counseling young girls who are going through difficult times. I'm proud to know you.

Dear Mister Rogers,
What's the best part about doing Mister Rogers' Neighborhood?

Adam, age 12

Dear Adam,
The best part of our work is being able to communicate with children and adults. Helping them know that they are unique and valuable human beings is one of the most important things about our program. It is especially good to hear from our "television friends" of all ages through the mail.

Dear Mister Rogers,
What is the hardest part of doing the program?
Jamilla, a college student

Dear Jamilla,

. . . I do enjoy working on our program, but, of course, as with any kind of work, we have some frustrating times. Often those are when we have problems with the equipment when we're taping in the studio. It can also be frustrating when I am trying to write something and can't seem to get an idea that feels right. In all work there are things we have to try hard to do—just like you're doing at school.

Sometimes, when I'm working on a script or composing a song, writing flows easily, but there are lots of times it doesn't. It's probably true that all writers have frustrating and discouraging moments. Sometimes it helps me to get away from the work—by taking a walk, sitting in a quiet room, listening to music, talking with a friend. Sometimes I just go over to the piano and play out my feelings through music. That kind of break seems to nourish me, and I can come back renewed. Sometimes it helps if I let someone else look at the writing and tell me what he or she thinks about it and what I might do to make it better. Or, if I set the writing down and come back to it another time, I often find new ways to express an old idea or even new ideas to express.

Dear Mister Rogers,
Where do you get your ideas?
                    Cambria, age 13

Dear Cambria,

. . . I write all of the scripts for our programs, but I
find ideas for the scripts in lots of different ways. You
may have the same experience we have, Cambria,
when you want to make a picture or a project and
find that your ideas can come from many places.
Sometimes we get ideas from the letters we've received
and sometimes from conversations with other people.
Sometimes our programs develop from things that
happen in our personal lives. For example, in our
week about NO & YES, we had a wedding in Make-
Believe, and I wrote that at the time our older son was
getting married. Even though I write the scripts for
our programs, I have a lot of good help from the
other people who work on the Neighborhood and
from other friends.

Dear Mister Rogers,
Do you like being famous?
            Junaid, age 10

Dear Junaid,
. . . That's a difficult question for me to answer,
because I don't think of myself as being a famous
person; I think of myself as a person who cares about
children and families. Since my work is on television,
many people know me and recognize me when they
see me. Sometimes people stop to talk to me, and I'm
always honored and glad to meet them. Of course, I
need to have private times, too, quiet times with my
family, my friends, and myself.

Dear Mister Rogers,
Do you get nervous?
        Brandon, age 10

Dear Brandon,
. . . It was difficult for me to do our programs at first,
Brandon, but instead of thinking of a large group of
people, I just think of one person who might be

watching, like you, and I imagine myself talking to that one person. That has helped me feel more comfortable with my work over the years.

Dear Mister Rogers,
Is Mister Rogers just a part that you act or is it the
real you?

Meaghan, age 10

Dear Meaghan,
. . . I don't think of myself as an actor, but as a person who likes to communicate with children. Television gives me a way to communicate with lots of children about their everyday concerns and about the things that interest them. I like to think of myself as a "television friend" for the children who are watching our program. Also, since I write the scripts, what I'm offering on our program is a natural part of who I am.

❀ When we care about people, we want to know more about them. Knowing what someone is like can help us feel closer. That's why I appreciate questions in the mail that children ask about me and my family.

Whether we're young or old, our questions generally reflect what's important in our own lives. For example, recognizing the importance of family to young children, it's understandable that many of them want to know about my family and my home. I also remember a mother who added a note to her son's question about what kind of car I drive, telling us that her son was going through a phase of being particularly fascinated with cars.

Likewise, I'd venture a guess that those questions about what I do when I'm angry or if I ever got in trouble when I was a boy came from children who were struggling to control their own angry feelings and negative urges. Developing that inner control is one of the tasks of childhood—and one that we continue to rework all through our lives! It's no wonder children are curious about other people and how they handle upsetting times.

CHAPTER THREE

Does it ever rain in your Neighborhood?

(Derek, age 4)

Dear Mister Rogers,
Do you live there?
> *Dana, age 5*

Dear Dana,
. . . I don't live in the television house. That is set up in our television studio. . . . My family and I live somewhere else in a real home. . . . When I finish taping each visit, I usually return to my office, which is in the same building as the studio. Then at the end of our workday, I return to my real home to spend time with my family.

Dear Mister Rogers,
Why aren't there any locks on your door?
> *Jason, age 3*

Dear Jason,

. . . That is because it's not a real house. I think of it
as my television house, where I stop by during my
workday to have a visit with my television friends. It is
set up in a big room at the television station so that
we can make our programs in a place that feels like a
house. In my real home, where I live with my family,
we do have locks and keys for the doors. In real
homes, locks and keys often help people feel safe.

Dear Mister Rogers,
I always wondered why you change your shoes and
sweater.

Katie, age 13

Dear Katie,

. . . I think of our program as a "television visit."
During my workday, I stop by at the "television
house" to have some time with our viewers. Because
I'm coming from my office, I'm wearing a jacket and
shoes that I'd wear at work. But I think of our visits as
a relaxing time with the children who are watching,

and changing to a sweater and sneakers helps set that comfortable atmosphere.

Dear Mister Rogers,
Do you zip your coat all the way up when you go
outside to play in the snow? Or do you leave the zipper
down a little like you do on your sweater? I want to
wear my coat just like you do. I think you leave your
zipper down a little. My mother thinks you zip your coat
all the way up. Please tell us what you do. Thank you
very much.

John, age 3

Dear John,
. . . You wanted to know why I zipper my sweaters only halfway up. I do that when we're making our television visits. That's because clipped to my tie is a microphone which helps people hear my voice through the television. Because the microphone is attached to the middle of my tie, which is the best place for the sound, I have to remember to lower the zipper on my sweater so it doesn't cover the microphone.

It might also help you to know that we make our

television program in a big room called a television studio. It's indoors, and it's warm there. So I'm warm enough if my sweater is just zipped up halfway. But when I go outside on a cold day, I zip my sweater or jacket up all the way so that I can be warm.

Staying warm is an important part of taking care of ourselves. It's good that your mother is helping you know about keeping warm. She cares about you, and she wants you to be healthy. I care about you, too, but I can be only a television friend. Until children are able to take care of themselves, it's good that they have grown-ups in their family who help them with that.

Dear Mister Rogers,
Why do you toss your shoe?
Alecia, age 10

Dear Alecia,
One day I was in an especially playful mood when our visit began, and I tossed my shoe. It was fun, and it's become a kind of game between Mr. Costa, our musical director and pianist, and me. He tries to play certain notes on the piano just as I catch my shoe.

Sometimes we do it together just right, and sometimes we don't, but it's fun for us to try each time because it's like a game. . . . I am very careful not to toss my shoe too high. I don't want to break anything.

Dear Mister Rogers,
Where is your computer?
                        Rafi, age 4

Dear Rafi,
. . . When I write scripts, I write with a pen on a long yellow notepad, and that's what's most comfortable for me. I don't use a computer at my work. But I am interested in the ways the people in our office use computers to help them with their work. Computers can be useful machines, especially when they help people communicate in caring ways with each other, like you did in your letter to me.

Dear Mister Rogers,
Does it ever rain in your neighborhood?
                              Rebecca, age 4

Dear Rebecca,
Our television Neighborhood is set up inside, in a big room called a television studio. Of course, it doesn't rain inside, but we sometimes make it look like it's raining. It takes a lot of work to make it look like it's raining in the studio, and we don't do that very often. But once in a while we do. I like to talk with my television friends about different kinds of weather. I know it's not always a "beautiful day" outside, but I like to think we can make it a "beautiful day" inside because we enjoy having a television visit together.

Dear Mister Rogers,
I want to know why you have a stoplight in your front room.

                              Carma, age 4

Dear Carma,

A long time ago, when we first started our program, we got a stoplight from the police department because we wanted to use it as a fun way for pretending to go to the rooms inside King Friday's Castle, like the M Room for Music or the G Room for the Gym. We pretended to go there by watching the green light blink thirteen times (for King Friday the Thirteenth). Now we usually say "Let's make believe. . . ."

Even though we don't use the stoplight to make believe about going to the Castle rooms, we thought it might be something interesting to keep in the living room of my television house. We use it now and then to talk about traffic lights on streets and keeping safe while crossing the street. I want my television friends to learn when they can or cannot cross the streets. I want them to be safe.

Dear Mister Rogers,
What is the purpose of feeding the fish every day? To demonstrate responsibility?

Meaghan, age 10

Dear Meaghan,

There are a few reasons why we feed the fish every day. First of all, when we feed the fish, we're showing that we "take care of" other living things, and being taken care of is something very important to children. They know they need grown-ups to provide them with food, like the fish in our tank need us to feed them. It does have a lot to do with responsibility, as you mentioned. I also like to watch anything that swims!

❀ One girl and her family wrote to tell us there was a special reason why she wanted me to talk about feeding the fish each day.

Dear Mister Rogers,
Please say when you are feeding your fish, because I worry about them. I can't see if you are feeding them, so please say you are feeding them out loud.
                                            Katie, age 5
(Father's note: Katie is blind, and she does cry if you don't say that you have fed the fish.)

❀ Since hearing from Katie, I've tried to remember to mention out loud those times that I'm feeding the fish. Over the years, I've learned so much from children and their families. I like to think that we've all grown together.

Dear Mister Rogers,
Why do you use a trolley?
        Kevin, age 11

Dear Kevin,
. . . There are a couple of reasons for that. First of all, we wanted to have a way of separating our Neighborhood (where things happen in a real way) from Make-Believe (where things can happen by pretending or by magic). Secondly, we wanted to show that we could all go together to another place—the Neighborhood of Make-Believe—by pretending. And, thirdly, I suppose I decided to use a trolley on our program because when I was growing up here in Pennsylvania, there were a lot of trolleys, and when I was a boy I liked taking rides on them.

Dear Mister Rogers,
How do you get the magic from the Trolley to go into
Make-Believe, and how do you make the Trolley come
back?

Miriam, age 4½

Dear Mister Rogers,
Please tell me how the Trolley goes from your house to
the Neighborhood of Make-Believe.

George, age 5

Dear Neighbor,
When we make our program the Trolley doesn't go immediately from the television house into Make-Believe. Actually, we produce the Make-Believe parts and the parts in my television house on different days. We videotape each part, and then our editor carefully puts the two parts together. So you see, the way we use the Trolley is a kind of pretending that happens through television.

❁ Often on our program, we've "demystified" things. I think it's important to be honest with children in that way. One adult was surprised by that and asked:

Dear Mister Rogers,
Why did you show the Trolley controls?
                    Mark, age 20

Dear Mark,
One of the best things about doing a television series
over many years is the opportunity to grow in our
work, and as I've learned more and developed in my
work, I've been able to rethink some of the ways we've
approached things in the past.

It was in the mid-1970s that we decided to show
the Trolley controls in my television house, and that's
because I felt it would be helpful for children to know
that machines like trolleys don't operate independently
of people. I think it's important to emphasize for
children that it's *people* who make machines work,
especially because young children have a hard time
understanding what's real and what's pretend. We've
talked about both the Trolley controls and the
"Picture-Picture" machine. We've even shown our
viewers the whole studio on certain occasions because
I think it's healthy to demystify this medium of
television as much as we can.

Dear Mister Rogers,
Why won't you go in the Make-Believe?
                    Dana, age 4½

Dear Dana,
. . . I decided not to be seen in Make-Believe because I think of myself as someone who is sitting with my television friends and listening to what's happening in that other pretend Neighborhood. Also, since I talk for many of the puppets in Make-Believe, it would be almost impossible to be there talking with them. I'm not a ventriloquist—the kind of puppeteer that doesn't move his or her mouth when making the puppet talk.

Dear Mister Rogers,
On one show I saw Mr. McFeely in your neighborhood
house, and then he was in Make-Believe. Did he get
there through the tunnel?

                              Alison, age 4

Dear Alison,
. . . We think of the Neighborhood of Make-Believe as a place we use for pretending. So anything can happen there. We can decide what the pretending will be like,

just as you decide about your pretending when you play and make things up. Well, in the Neighborhood of Make-Believe, we pretend that it's just the Trolley that goes through the tunnel. And we pretend that the other people, like Mr. McFeely, Handyman Negri, Betty Aberlin, and Chef Brockett can get there any way they want. Anything's possible in Make-Believe!

You might want to make up a story or draw about a fun way that Mr. McFeely or the others could get to Make-Believe. Children can have very good ideas for their pretending.

Dear Mister Rogers,
I have a question, does Henrietta Pussycat have a mommy and a daddy?

                                              Sara, age 3¼

Dear Sara,
In the Neighborhood of Make-Believe we pretend that Henrietta is young, like a child. If she were a real child, she would need a parent to take care of her, just as you need grown-ups to help take care of you until

you're old enough to take care of yourself. But
Henrietta isn't real. She's a puppet, and so we can
pretend about her any way we want. When we
pretend, things can be any way we want them to be.
You might want to have your own pretend about
Henrietta's family. You might even want to make your
own puppets and play about it.

Dear Mister Rogers,
Why aren't there hands on Daniel's clock?
                                    Joe, toddler

Dear Joe,
. . . I'm glad that you enjoy our television visits and
that you wanted to ask me a question about Daniel's
clock. We decided not to have any hands on Daniel's
clock because his clock is in the Neighborhood of
Make-Believe, and that's a place where we pretend
things can be any way we want them to be. We
decided that we would pretend there was no time in
Make-Believe, like the timelessness of love. If you were
making up a pretend place, what kinds of things would

you have there? Would you have hands on your pretend clock? For your pretending, things can be any way you want them to be!

Dear Mister Rogers,
Where did your ideas for the puppets come from? Why is Daniel scared and shy?

Courtney, age 5

Dear Courtney,
Ideas for Make-Believe come from many different places, just like ideas for your own pretending do. Some of our puppets were a part of a television program I helped to make in the 1950s (a local Pittsburgh WQED children's program called *Children's Corner*). It's hard to say where the ideas for a puppet's personality come from. How the puppet looks to you, as well as how you feel at the moment or what a story is about, helps decide. We all have feelings of being scared and shy sometimes. I know that's a part of children's feelings, and I remember feeling that way when I was a boy.

The first time I put Daniel Striped Tiger on my hand was the very first day of *Children's Corner*.

Maybe feeling nervous and shy that day were very real feelings for me, and so Daniel may have been a way to express that shyness. There are probably times when we all feel like Lady Elaine—adventurous and mischievous—or like King Friday—wanting to be in charge—or like Daniel—scared and shy.

I wonder if you ever do some play with puppets. You might like to try with sock puppets or paper bag puppets. What you imagine or make would be unique because it came from you.

Dear Mister Rogers,
Why does King Friday have people say, "Correct as usual"?

Phillip, age 4

Dear Phillip,
When we make up our stories for Make-Believe, we think of King Friday as a kind king, but he's also someone who worries that people won't love him unless he's very important—and one way he feels important is by thinking he's always right. So we pretend he insists the Neighbors say, "Correct as usual" as a way of making them say, "You're right, King Friday, as you always are." Of course, no one is

always right! Certainly King Friday hasn't always been right. Pretending about King Friday that way can give us a chance to talk about some of the feelings we all have about people who need to feel important and to remember that we don't have to be right all the time in order to be loved.

❀ One mother wrote to thank us for the way we represented King Friday. Watching how the others relate to him, especially when he's been bullheaded, helped her son deal with the bullies in his real neighborhood!

Dear Mister Rogers,
Why is Lady Elaine in the Neighborhood of Make-Believe? . . . She's always in mischief. Maybe you should ask her to leave, or tell her "Don't do just anything you want."

Sarah, age 5

Dear Sarah,
Lady Elaine is a puppet, and she fits on my hand. I do the voice for her. And I write the stories about the Neighborhood of Make-Believe. That's a kind of pretending.

It is good that you wanted to let us know how you feel about Lady Elaine. Even though she sometimes gets into trouble, she has to find ways to fix the trouble, and often she feels sorry about what she's done. At times like that, Lady Elaine can help us understand that we can't just do anything we want. That is important learning, and I'm glad that's important to you.

Lady Elaine also gives us a way to help children think about how important everyone can be in a Neighborhood. She often adds adventure, mischief, pleasure, and fun in a way that others do not. You might want to make up your own stories about her.

Dear Mister Rogers,
Tell Lady Elaine . . . not to do mean things.
                              Kara, age 5

Dear Kara,
. . . Lady Elaine sometimes says things that hurt others' feelings. Usually she does things like that to feel important. But her friends let her know they care

about her and that she *is* an important part of the Neighborhood of Make-Believe—just by being herself. When she realizes she has done something unkind, she often lets her friends know she's sorry and tries to help them know about her feelings.

You might like to make up your own stories about what Lady Elaine would say when *she* reads your letter. . . . You might even want to make a "Lady Elaine Fairchilde" puppet of your own.

Dear Mister Rogers,
I would like to know why you do not turn off the lights when you leave your television house. You can turn them back on when you come back. Do you leave the lights on for Mr. McFeely?

Mark, age 4

Dear Neighbor,
The place where we have our television visits is not my real house. I think of it as my "television house," and it's set up in a television studio. I don't use the lights there like people do in a real home. When I enter, I

don't need to turn the lights on. In fact, the lights are in the ceiling of the television studio, and they help the television cameras show the pictures clearly.

When I'm in my real home, I do try to remember to turn off the lights when I leave a room or when I don't need them. That's an important rule for me and my family, too, and it's important for our world that we use lights and electricity caringly. It's good that your family cares about our world and is helping you know about rules like that. Mark, you are fortunate to be growing up in a family like yours.

Dear Mister Rogers,
Why don't you put your shoes back on at the end of the program? Do you go outside with your socks on?
                                                                Janae, age 4

Dear Janae,
. . . Other children have mentioned that, too, and I can understand that it looks like I don't put my shoes on when I go outside at the end of our program. The shoes that I wear when I come into the television house are loafers that I can easily slip out of before I

put the sneakers on. Because I usually sing a good-bye song at the end, the camera shows mainly my face, and it doesn't show what's happening on the floor where I'm slipping into the loafers while I'm singing. But I'm wearing them even if they aren't seen!

Dear Mister Rogers,
When you put on your coat and say good-bye, my three-year-old daughter, Meagan, always asks, "Where is he going, Mommy?"

At first I answered, "I don't know." Then, after several more times of asking, we decided to write to you and ask, "Where do you go?"

So, Mr. Rogers, where do you go when you say good-bye?

Meagan and Mommy

Dear Mrs. —— and Meagan,
When we first began making our programs, we were on the air at 5:00 P.M., which is the time I would normally be going home from work. I thought of my television house as a place where I stop by at the end of my workday, to have a television visit with children

before going home. Now, our programs are shown at different times of the day. So I think of my television house as a place where I stop by during my workday to have some time with my television friends, and then I either go up to the office for some more work, or if it's the end of the day, I go home to my family.

❀ One child's comment was such a warm indication of trust about our program's being a "television visit," where I stop to have some time with the children who are watching. I just loved what she said:

> *Dear Mister Rogers,*
> *Thank you for showing up when it's time for your show!*
> *Mirele, age 4*

❀ Bless her heart; I wonder what she thought would happen if I didn't "show up" on time!

When children watch television, they're bringing their whole lives with them. They're comparing what they see and hear on the screen to what they've experienced in their homes, at school, and in their inner beings.

Much of television can be confusing and upsetting for children—especially children who are dealing daily with the usual "worries and scareys" of growing up. That's why I've always believed the best way for children to watch anything on television is to have a caring adult nearby who can talk about the program with them and who can encourage them to say what they think about it and question what they don't understand—adults who will even share these things with those of us who produce the programs that the children see and hear.

CHAPTER FOUR

How long
is a minute?

(Alyssa, age 5)

Dear Mister Rogers,
We want to know why the leaves don't turn blue in
Autumn. I think they should turn blue because blue is
close to green. I am sending a picture of two blue leaves
on the ground.

Sarah, age 3

Dear Sarah,

. . . I don't understand much about leaves, but I do know that what makes the leaf green is the chlorophyll inside it. When the weather gets cooler, the chlorophyll doesn't work anymore, but that allows the other colors in the leaf to show. I guess that leaves can have only certain colors, like yellow, red, orange, and brown, and can't have other colors, like blue.

As you grow, you will have more ways of learning about leaves and colors and about the things you're wondering. You might want to ask your family to help you find a book about leaves in the library. Reading

books is another way to learn. . . . What's wonderful
about drawing or pretending or making up stories is
that you can make the leaves any color you want them
to be. Children have so many wonderful ideas for their
pretending.

Dear Mister Rogers,
I want to know how the world started. I think a star
exploded and then it got all the pieces of the star [and]
made the world. Sometimes I see a shape, like a circle
around us. It makes me think that a star exploded
because there looks like there's a circle around us and
when you look at stars they look like circles, too.
                                        Benjamin, age 4

Dear Benjamin,
. . . Many things about this world are hard to
understand—even for scientists. Since no one was
living on the earth when the world started, people
have tried for a long time to imagine what that was
like. They try to look and listen carefully to the earth
for clues about how things began, but they also
imagine.
    Imagination isn't just something children need for

their pretending—it's part of the work of grown people like scientists, too. Different people have different ideas about how the world started. I'm glad to know yours. It's good that you are trying to figure it out for yourself. That's a healthy way to keep growing all your life.

❀ Questions like that often come to us because children think of adults as all-knowing, all-wise. They think we know all the answers. It's okay that we don't have answers to some questions. Just applauding the question and listening to a child's opinions can be all the encouragement he or she needs.

One mother wrote to say:

Dear Mister Rogers,
. . . My son asked me why, if he was so special and nobody was exactly like him, were there three boys in his class with his name.

Mary Ann

Dear Adam,
. . . It's especially hard to understand that things can be alike in some ways, and different in other ways. It's that way for people. People can be alike in some ways

and different in other ways: like those boys in your
class. You're boys. You have the same first name.
You're in the same class. But you have different
families, different things that you like and don't like,
different friends, and many other things that are
different, even different *last* names. When I say,
"There's no one exactly like you," I mean that there's
no one who has *everything* exactly the same as you.

Learning about alike and different is an important
part of growing, and asking questions is one way to
help with that growing.

Dear Mister Rogers,
Why don't wishes come true? I got a troll with a star
but my wishes didn't come true. I want a horse but I
can't get it, because I don't have enough money, and
because I'm getting too much toys. What do you think
about it?

Leba, age 5

Dear Leba,

You asked me why wishes don't come true, and I can understand that you were disappointed when your troll with a star didn't make your wishes come true. I wonder if you know our song "Wishes Don't Make Things Come True"?* No kinds of wishes can make things come true.

Leba, dreaming and wishing by themselves don't make anything happen. It takes people to make things happen. Even though wishes can't come true, you might want to have your own play and pretending about your wishes. You told me you'd like to have a horse. You might want to make up stories or draw pictures about a horse or something else you'd like to have. For your pretending, things can be any way you want them to be. Also, you might want to find books in the library about horses. There are many things we can do when we can't have the things we want. In fact, whether we like it or not, everyone has to learn to deal with disappointment. That's one of the biggest things we ever learn to do. I'm proud of you for starting now.

* See page 140.

Dear Mister Rogers,
While shopping with my Mommy one day, I asked her if
they shot those chickens we were going to buy. She said
she was sure they didn't. So I asked her, "How does the
farmer get them to lie down?" Mommy said she didn't
know, but maybe Mister Rogers knew the answer.
Do you?

Eddie, age 3½

Dear Eddie,
You wanted to know if the farmers shot the chickens
and how they get them to lie down. That's a hard
thing to explain to you, but it may help to know that
farmers have special ways of doing that.

As you grow older, you will probably be able to
understand things like that, but even now it's good
that you're asking questions when you're wondering
about something. The adults in your life will do their
best to take care of you and to tell you the things they
feel you can understand. Talking with people who care
about you can help them know what you're
wondering. That's one important way for you to grow
and learn.

❀ Here's an excerpt from the letter we sent to Eddie's mother:

> Dear Mrs. ———,
> We were touched by Eddie's questions about the
> farmers and the chickens, and we can understand how
> difficult it is for parents to handle those kinds of
> questions. That uncomfortableness may come from an
> instinctual feeling that there are some things that
> three-and-a-half-year-olds are not ready to understand.
> Young children haven't lived long enough or
> experienced enough of the world to handle certain
> kinds of information. Although we have not specifically
> answered Eddie's question in our response to him, we
> have attempted to show respect for his concerns and
> his curiosity. Over time, this farmer question may
> come up again; and, if you feel he's old enough, you
> can then find other ways to help him understand.

> *Dear Mister Rogers,*
> *A few days ago my 3½-year-old asked about my cat. He*
> *wanted to know when she would have kittens. (We just*
> *had a new baby this year.) I told him that she would*

*never have kittens, and he asked why. WHY? What
could I possibly tell a young child about having spayed
my cat? I changed the subject. Could such a question
have been dealt with in a more direct way? How could I
tell a little boy about this without scaring him? Do you
know?*

Alison

Dear Mrs. ———,

. . . I can well understand your concerns about helping
your child know about your cat being spayed. As with
anything like that, it is often best to give a short and
simple answer. Children can't handle much
information at one time. And they will ask for more if
they feel they need it, and if we leave the door open
for discussion in the future.

A simple way to explain spaying might be that the
cat has had a special operation that can be done for
cats so the animal doesn't have babies. How wise of
you, though, to assume that the birth of *your* baby
may be what he's really questioning! He may be
wondering about how many more siblings *he* will have.
As with any other sensitive issue, probably the best

kind of help is to ask your child what he thinks about his question and about your answer. That is a good way to lead to more and more understanding.

❀ Here is one of the most touching letters we've received over the years. It's one that helps me realize how children can misinterpret things about our world that we adults often take for granted—things like *time*.

Dear Mister Rogers,

Our 5½-year-old daughter, Michelle, has an inoperable brain tumor. Our only hope to remove the tumor is with radiation. On the first day of her radiation treatment, she screamed and cried when she found out she would have to be in the room all by herself. She was so upset they could not give her the treatment.

The next day the doctor gave us some medication to sedate her. It was supposed to put her to sleep. By the time we reached the hospital, she was still wide awake. We all tried talking her into doing the treatment, but she cried again and said no. We kept saying that it would only take one minute—thirty seconds on each side.

Finally she asked me, "What is a minute?" I know it was by the grace of God that I thought of how to explain

*to her what was one minute. I looked at my watch and
started singing, "It's a beautiful day in this
neighborhood, a beautiful day for a neighbor . . ." and
before I could finish the song I said, "Oops! The minute
is up. I can't even finish Mr. Rogers' song." Then
Michelle said, "Is that a minute? I can do that." And
she did. She laid perfectly still for the entire treatment;
but, there was a catch to it. I have to sing your song
every time over the intercom into the treatment room. It
is very embarrassing but I do it gladly for her. By now,
every doctor and technician in Radiation Therapy knows
your song.*

Michelle's Mom

❀ We can't always know what's behind a child's question.
But if we let a child know we respect the question, we're
letting that child know we respect him or her. What a powerful way to say, "I care about you!"

Questions are one of the most essential things children
bring to their learning. *Wanting* to know about something
is the first step of wanting to give the energy to learning
more about it. When we caringly respond to children's questions, we're encouraging curiosity, which is a tool they'll
need for their learning all throughout their lives.

Asking questions gives a child a way to make a connection with another person. It can be a beginning step toward reaching out, communicating, and building a relationship. So when we applaud their questions, we're encouraging children's social development.

At the same time, answering questions that come in the mail can be more frustrating than ones that come in person. I don't really know the child who is asking. Often I don't even know the age of the child or anything about the child's family or life situation . . . or what came before the question . . . or what might be behind the question. What's more, I can't see that child's face when I respond, so I don't have cues about how that child is reacting, to know how much or how little to offer. But I have always believed that it's important to be as honest as we possibly can be when children ask a question (in person or in the mail) and that the most important part of our answer is in applauding the very act of questioning.

That's why I often end our answers with a statement like: *I'm proud to have a television friend like you who wonders about things and who asks questions about what you're wondering. Wondering and asking questions are important for growing and learning.*

CHAPTER FIVE

Sometimes it's
hard to behave

Me

7½ years

Eric

8 years

Dear Mr Rogers I'm facing something so difficult
I feel sad and Broken your such a Good friend I'd lik
some help. My BEST friend is having a 99% chan
of Moving I don't know when. This morning in class he
told me when I Got home I I cryed a lot then I knew
you could help me so I hope and trust you will

your televison neighbor,

Brent

(Brent, age 7½)

Dear Mister Rogers,

. . . My best friend Eric is having a 99% chance of moving. I don't know when. This morning in class he told me. When I got home I cryed a lot. . . .

Brent, age 7½

Dear Brent,

Your letter meant so much to me. I was really touched that you felt I could help you at such an upsetting time. I certainly can understand how hard it must be for you to consider Eric's moving away.

Brent, there are no easy ways to handle those feelings. What often helps is to talk about what we're feeling. Somehow, talking about feelings can make them more manageable. That doesn't mean talking about problems can make the problems go away. Far from that! Sad and angry feelings about a friend moving away can hurt us deep inside. What I was most proud of in your letter is that you are a person who can talk about what you're feeling.

Generally, when we've been through sad times and we've been able to think and talk about our feelings, we usually begin to feel better, little by little. That's like the words in our song, ". . . the very same people who are sad sometimes . . . are the very same people who are glad sometimes. It's funny but it's true . . . It's the same, isn't it, for me and you. . . ."

Something else that might help is to plan ways that you and Eric could stay in touch. I know of friends who have been separated, but who continue to stay in touch by writing or phoning or visiting on holidays or birthdays. Eric can continue to be an important part of who you are, even though he may not live nearby . . . just as you and I can be "television neighbors" even though we don't actually live near each other. Your friendship with Eric will always be an important part of who you are. And your friendship will always be an important part of who Eric is, too.

Brent, I also wanted to mention that, as I read your letter, I couldn't help but think what a gifted communicator you are! You use words so well to talk about what you're thinking and feeling. And I liked the way you helped me know more about yourself and

Eric through your drawings. I'm proud to know you.
You are special!

Dear Mister Rogers,
I'm being really good and behaving at school and home.
Sometimes it's hard to behave.

Danny, age 6

Dear Danny,
You're a fine boy, Danny, and I was pleased to get to
know you through all that you told me in your letter.
You're six years old, and you'll soon be in
kindergarten. Danny, you also told me that you're
working hard to be good at home and at school, but
that sometimes it's hard to behave. I can understand
that. One of our songs has the words "Good people
sometimes do bad things, once in a while we do."*
What's important is that you're *trying* to behave. I'm
proud of you for all the times when you've been able
to control yourself when you felt like misbehaving. I
hope you're proud of these times, too. I call that
"inside growing," and I like the way you're growing—
inside and out.

* See page 20.

Dear Mister Rogers,

My daughter Caitlin, who is three years old, had an upsetting experience today and asked me to write to you. We were on our way to the park and ran into her grandfather who was watching some buildings being demolished. We stopped to say hello and watch with him. Caitlin stood by us while I chatted and watched the activity across the street. A few minutes went by before Caitlin broke into sobbing tears. I picked her up, and she buried her head in my neck saying she didn't want to see them "tearing down houses." . . . While we were at the playground she asked many questions about tearing down houses. I tried to reassure her by telling her there was no one in them, that they were going to build something new, etc. After some silence she looked at me very seriously and said, "Maybe Mr. Rogers could talk about tearing down houses."

Caitlin and her Mommy

Dear Caitlin,

It meant a great deal to me that you wanted your mother to write and tell me about the day you saw the people tearing down the houses. I can understand how that might be upsetting for you. Houses are very important to people. It can be scary to think that someone might be tearing down a house that belongs to a family.

Caitlin, your own house is a safe place, and your mother and father will do all they can to keep you safe and to keep your home safe. No one will tear down your house while your family needs it.

It's good that you told your mother about your worries and that she helped you understand more about why people tear down houses—and that people would not tear down a house that a family needs.

It was interesting to know you wanted me to talk about that on our television visits. Maybe we will someday. I'm always glad to know what my television friends would like us to show or talk about.

There are a lot of things in this world that are hard to understand, and I'm glad you can talk about your feelings with the grown-ups in your family. Your mother cares about you, Caitlin, and she obviously cares about what you're feeling.

Dear Mister Rogers,
There is this boy at school and he said girls can't play
basketball. What should I do?

Marie, age 8

Dear Marie,

Thank you for writing to me about your problem with
the boy who told you girls can't play basketball. I'm
proud that you are someone who can talk about the
things that are upsetting you.

Marie, I think girls can play whatever sports they
want to play. So can boys. One time on our program
we had a visit with Suzie McConnell, who was a
member of the U.S. women's basketball team that won
the gold medal in the 1988 Olympics.

When we are upset by something, I believe that the
best kind of help comes from people who can know us
in a real and everyday kind of way . . . people we feel
comfortable with and who are good listeners. I wonder
if you might want to talk about your feelings about
what that boy said with someone in your family or at
school. I have always called talking about feelings
"important talk."

✤ A few weeks later, Marie sent us a drawing of herself smiling and holding a basketball in her hands.

Dear Mister Rogers,
Why does G.I. Joe shoot and punch the bad guys? My
mom says that's not a good way to fix things . . . I'm
not sure about it. What do you think about it?

Peter, age 4

Dear Peter,
. . . I was glad to see that you and your mom had some important talk about "bad guys" on television. Television shows like that are a kind of pretending. They have stories about getting rid of "bad guys." Children often like those kinds of stories because they like to think that "good guys" will keep people safe from "bad guys."

But, in real life, there are no "good guys" who are always good, and there are no "bad guys" who are always bad. Most people try to be good, but they do bad things once in a while. We made up a song about that ("Good People Sometimes Do Bad Things"*), and I'm sending you the words to it. Maybe you and your

* See page 20.

mom will talk about what that song means to your family.

Some children like to pretend about getting rid of the "bad guys." Of course in real life there are much better ways we can help people who do bad things. Even when people do "bad" things, they still need people to care about them and their feelings. Real life is different from pretend. I hope you and your family will talk more about things like what's real and what's pretend, what happens when people do good things, and what happens when they do bad things. That's important talk.

Dear Mister Rogers,
Thank you for telling me robots don't have feelings.
Bikes, trees, and balloons don't have feelings either; only people, right?

Jared, age 5

❀ Can you hear a sense of relief in that child's statement? It's a wonderful example of how helpful it is to let children know that machines, like our Trolley and robots, don't have feelings and needs like human beings and animals do. Machines are different from people. Demystifying doesn't kill children's appreciation of something; it can give them an even greater appreciation of the people who invented and developed those things.

Dear Mister Rogers,
I am starting to lose my first tooth. It's wiggling a lot.
Darren, age 6

Dear Darren,
It was interesting to know you have a loose tooth, and it meant a lot to me that you wanted to share that news with me. Children can have different feelings about losing a tooth. Sometimes it can be annoying to have a tooth that wiggles. When the tooth falls out, it can feel like you've lost something that's been with you as long as you can remember. Some children find they can't bite into some foods as easily as they could before, until the new tooth grows in. There can also be some exciting feelings, because having a loose tooth is one sign that you're growing. Your baby teeth start to become loose to make room for the bigger teeth to come in. I'm proud of the many ways you're growing, and I hope you are, too.

Dear Mister Rogers,
I don't wet my bed anymore.
                    Stephen, age 4

I went to the toilet—and Mister Rogers is gonna be so
proud of me—let's find out where he is . . . I have dry
pants now. Tell him how old I am—and tell him how I
spell my name. (Mother's note: Joey is 3 years old and
he spells his name JOSEPH—and he draws all by
himself.) I don't wear diapers anymore.
                    Dictated to Mommy by Joey, age 3

Dear Neighbor,

. . . I liked the letter about how excited you were that
you have dry pants and that you don't wear diapers
anymore. It meant a lot to me that you wanted to tell
me that. I know that it is hard to learn to keep dry,
and that the very same people who are dry sometimes
are the very same people who are wet sometimes.

I'm proud of you! I'm glad you're proud, too!

Dear Mister Rogers,

My name is Luke and I'm three years old. I'm writing to tell you about something I did that was very hard for me to do. Ever since the beginning of summer, I've been trying my hardest to potty train. Today, I finally made a bowel movement in the toilet for the first time! My whole family was very excited. I got to have ice cream with chocolate chips on it. My mom promised me that I could send a letter to you if I made a bowel movement in the toilet. So, here is my letter.

Luke, age 3

Dear Luke,

It meant a lot to me that you wanted to write and tell me you made a bowel movement in the toilet for the first time! That is exciting news. I know how hard it can be to learn to use the toilet. I also know that when you're just learning about something like using the toilet, there can be some times when you have an "accident." I hope you can feel good about yourself for all the times that you manage well with that and that you can understand nobody is perfect—especially when you're learning something new!

It was fun to read in your letter about how your

family celebrated with you. Your family is proud of you. I'm proud of you. And it's good to know you're proud, too! That's such a good feeling!

❋ It's a real gift when a child can put his or her feelings into words—whether those feelings are painful or exciting. When I answer letters in which children have shared their feelings with me, I like to let them know that they are not alone with their feelings, that there are other children (and adults) who have those kinds of feelings, and to let them know that there are people who care. Isn't that what most of us human beings want when we're ready to share what's inside?

CHAPTER SIX

I am scared
of spiders
and monsters

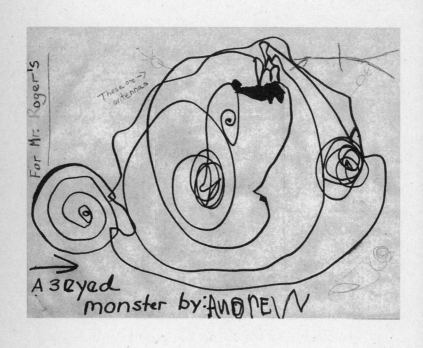

(Andrew, age 5)

Dear Mister Rogers,
My name is Hannah. I am four years old, but I am
afraid of the dark. Could you talk about that worry on
your show?

Hannah, age 4

Dear Hannah,
It's good that you could tell me that you are afraid of
the dark. I know that lots of children are afraid of the
dark, and I also know there are some things that can
help.

When children are afraid, it can help to talk with
the grown-ups in their family. Sometimes it helps to
play about what is scary or draw pictures or make up
stories or play with puppets. If it's bedtime, you might
like to have some quiet stories or soft music just
before you go to sleep. You might even like to have
something in bed with you, like a cuddly stuffed
animal. Even though some things can help, it takes a

while to manage scary feelings. Little by little, we can feel better about what was scary for us. It's a part of inside growing to be able to talk about what you're feeling. I'm proud of the many ways you're growing, and I hope you are, too. You are special—just because you're you.

Dear Mister Rogers,
I am scared of spiders and monsters. They come into my bedroom and on my seat in my car. . . . I have monster spray, Mister Rogers. I use it everywhere in my room. It helps keep the monsters and spiders out. I am helping myself by using the spray. I can just help myself! . . . What can I do to stop being scared of monsters and spiders?

John, age 3

Dear John,
It meant a lot to me that you wanted to tell me your feelings about spiders and monsters. Many boys and girls are scared about things like that. It was interesting to know you pretend to be able to spray the monsters and spiders with your pretend monster spray. Playing

and pretending about things that scare you can
sometimes help. That way, you can be in charge of the
scary things. Sometimes it helps to draw, too, and . . .
I wondered if it might help you to draw about some
of the things that scare you. Little by little, as you
grow, some of the things that upset you now won't be
as scary. That's a part of inside growing. And I'm
proud of the many ways you're growing—inside
and out.

❁ One child sent us a complex drawing with these words
on it:

Dear Mister Rogers,
I put scary writing on it.
            Paul, age 4

Dear Paul,
You certainly had some interesting ideas for the
drawing you sent me. You told me it was a road with
waterfalls and some scary writing on it that looked like
dinosaur teeth. It meant a lot to me that you wanted
to share that picture with me. It's good that you want

to draw about all kinds of things, even scary ones. Drawing and talking about the things you're thinking and feeling are good ways to grow.

Dear Mister Rogers,
Did you get dressed up on Halloween? I was a skeleton and I scared people.

Bob, age 5

Dear Bob,
When I was a boy, I liked to dress up in costumes. Sometimes my friends and I would make costumes and put on plays. Dressing up can be such a good way to pretend about things. I liked to wear costumes on Halloween, too. On Halloween, children can pretend about all sorts of things—even about scaring people, like you did in your skeleton costume. When you pretended to be a skeleton, you made the skeleton do what *you* wanted it to do, and you were in charge of making the skeleton just as scary as *you* wanted it to be. Pretending like that also helps you know that other walking, talking skeletons that you may see are only make-believe.

Dear Mister Rogers,
A couple of months ago one of your shows featured a
make-believe story involving the wind. In it, I believe
Purple Panda was blown away. . . . My daughter,
Rebecca, age 3, has since been afraid of letting go of my
hand outside if there is a slight breeze. As time goes by, I
think the story idea just grows in her mind.

Rebecca's mother

Dear Mrs. ———,

Thank you for being in touch with us. We care deeply
about the children and families who are watching, and,
naturally, we were sorry to know about your
daughter's reaction to one of our programs.

From what you told us about Rebecca's fear, I
wonder if the program was our opera, *Windstorm in
Bubbleland*. We thought it may help you to have some
information about that, which we've enclosed. It's hard
to understand how children may interpret something,
but I want to assure you that we wouldn't have had
any character, even Purple Panda, blown away by the
wind, because we know how scary that could be for
young children. That story was an opera which took
place in the Neighborhood of Make-Believe, an area

we refer to as a kind of pretending, and it was about the Neighbors working together to control the wind.

During that program, we gave extra care to our discussions about the wind. But, as caring as we may be, any particular segment may evoke something that's upsetting to a child. And, as well as parents know their child, it can sometimes be difficult to know what may be causing a certain reaction.

I can imagine how hard it must be for you to watch your daughter struggle with her fear of the wind. Of course, it's your ongoing loving support that will be the most important thing to her as she tries to manage her worries about wind or whatever else may be of concern to her.

❀ Here is part of the letter we sent Rebecca:

Dear Rebecca,
. . . I'm glad to know that we're television friends, but I was sorry to know that one of our programs was scary for you.

It's good that you can talk about the things on television that are scary for you, and it's good that your mother wrote to tell us how you felt. It can help to talk about feelings—whether they're sad or scary or angry or happy. I call that important talk.

Rebecca, we talked about the wind on one of our operas, *Windstorm in Bubbleland*, and I wonder if that was the program that was scary for you. All our operas are pretend. In fact, that's how I think about Make-Believe—it's a place where we can pretend about things. In that opera, Lady Elaine was dressed as a hummingbird, and we pretended that the windstorm was strong and that she couldn't fly in it. But her friends worked together to find a way to make the windstorm stop, and then she was fine.

There's a story about our *Windstorm in Bubbleland* opera which I'm sending for your mother. Maybe she could talk about it with you. I also know that when something is frightening, it can take a while before you feel better about it.

❀ Here are excerpts from our writings that we sent:

We all carry "inner dramas" within us, all our lives. We bring them to everything we see and do. For instance, if we'd been bitten by a dog when we were very young, we may have anxious feelings—at some level of our being—whenever we see a dog. Most of us, though, as we grow older, find our own ways of coping with stressful feelings like that. In fact, one of the important tasks in growing up is to develop healthy ways to cope.

If you've watched *Mister Rogers' Neighborhood*, you probably know that our programs do not try to avoid anxiety-arousing situations. We have dealt with the beginnings of life, as well as with its end, and with many of the feelings in between. We do try, though, to keep anxiety within a child's manageable limits and then to deal with it. We talk about those feelings and, in simple ways, try to show models for coping with them as well as models of trustworthy, caring, and available adults.

. . . The inner dramas of early childhood are perhaps the hardest for us adults to understand. They are subtle and deep; and, of course, young children do not have the concepts or words yet to talk very clearly about them. For our part, we are so far from them that most of us can't remember what they were. But they are there, a part of every child, and somewhere, a part of us. That's why I feel that those of us who make television programs—for adults or for children—have a responsibility to do our work with the greatest of care. Those of us who are parents have an equally great responsibility for knowing what our children are watching and for helping them cope with the inner dramas those programs may arouse.

I don't believe I've ever met a child who didn't have some fears about something while growing up—nor parents who weren't concerned about what to do about them.

. . . Sometimes children may be afraid of things that do what they, themselves, are trying to learn *not* to do. Most children pass through a stage when they have an urge to bite, for instance, and when they're trying to master that urge, they can be very frightened of things that can or do bite.

. . . We can often guess what's bothering children when they allow us to watch their play, when they're drawing or pretending, or making up stories. And we can encourage them to go on playing about their feelings, too. The more they can handle scary things in their play, the less scary such things need to seem everywhere else.

. . . Sometimes children develop unaccountable fears of things that aren't real—at least not in the way adults perceive "reality." . . . There are many times when parents can't solve their children's problems. Perhaps all they can do is to provide a safe, loving place and a willingness to listen and talk while the children work through whatever is bothering them. That's what I call "being there," and far from being a passive, helpless role, this is often the most active and helpful kind of support parents can give.

❀ Children who have to undergo painful medical experiences often have remarkable courage. We hear now and then about how brave they've been. Those letters have been especially touching.

Dear Mister Rogers,
I fell and got stitches in my head. I was a big boy and I was very brave.

David, age 4½

Dear Mister Rogers,
One day I got hurt and had to go to the hospital. . . . I slipped and cut my foot . . . and it hurt. I got stitches . . . and I had to have my pink blanket, and my teddy, and Daddy stayed with me in the hospital.

Sarah, age 4

Dear Neighbor,

It meant a great deal to me that you wanted to write and tell me about the time you were hurt and had to go to the hospital. I am sorry that your foot was hurting, but it is good that there are people at hospitals who know how to help children when they have a problem like that. And the best part is when you can come home from the hospital.

It was interesting to hear about what helped you when you were in the hospital. You said you had your pink blanket and your teddy there, and that your daddy stayed with you in the hospital. It does help to have special things from home and the people you care about close to you at times like that. You are growing so well—inside and out. I'm proud of you.

Dear Mister Rogers,
My name is Alex, I am 4 and I have leukemia. I am
very brave with my needles and chemo.

Alexandria, age 4

Dear Alex,

. . . That's a good feeling—to know you are brave. I can understand there can be a lot of times when it's hard to be brave, especially when you have leukemia. There can even be angry and scary times, too. I wonder what helps you at times like that? It can often help to talk about what's hard for you with your family and with the doctors and nurses or other people at the hospital. It can also help to draw pictures or make up stories.

❀ Over the years we've had a number of letters from Alex, and in the latest one, she told us things are going well for her.

Dear Mister Rogers,
Just to let you know, I am in full remission and have
NO sign of cancer in my body what so ever. I have
grown up a lot since I last wrote to you.
*   —Alexandria, age 9*

CHAPTER SEVEN

My brother copies
everything
I do

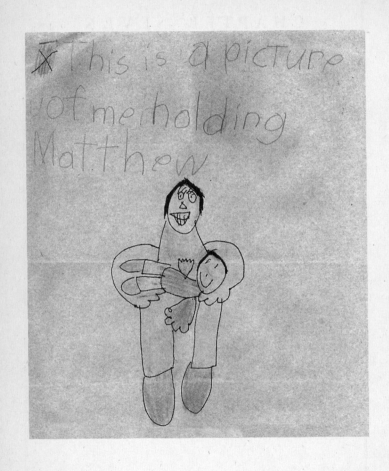

This is a picture of me holding Matthew

(Mary, age 7)

Dear Mister Rogers,
The baby came to live at my house. I like her sometimes.
Sometimes I want to sock her.

Taylor, age 3

*(Mother's note: Taylor wanted to know if you could send
a picture of yourself angry.)*

Dear Taylor,
. . . You told me about the new baby at your house
and that sometimes you like her and sometimes you
don't. It's good that you can talk about your feelings,
whether you're happy or sad or angry. That's
important talk. What you told me reminded me of our
song, "What Do You Do?" I wondered what *you* do
when you feel angry—that doesn't hurt anyone or ruin
anything.

What Do You Do?

What do you do with the mad that you feel
When you feel so mad you could bite?
When the whole wide world seems oh so wrong,
And nothing you do seems very right?
What do you do? Do you punch a bag?
Do you pound some clay or some dough?
Do you round up friends for a game of tag?
Or see how fast you go?

It's great to be able to stop
When you've planned a thing that's wrong,
And be able to do something else instead
And think this song:

I can stop when I want to,
Can stop when I wish,
Can stop, stop, stop anytime.
And what a good feeling to feel like this,
And know that the feeling is really mine.
Know that there's something deep inside
That helps us become what we can.
For a girl can be someday a woman,
And a boy can be someday a man.

Taylor, you asked if we could send you a picture of me looking angry. We don't have any like that. But I certainly do get angry sometimes; everybody does. We all have our own way of saying that we're angry. Playing the piano loud and swimming very fast help me with my mad feelings.

You have a special place in your family, Taylor, and so does your sister. You will always be the older one. There's only one person in the whole world exactly like you, and the people who care about you can like you just because you're you.

Dear Mister Rogers,
Melissa is a baby sister of mine but her nickname is Missy. I like her but sometimes I get mad at her like when she cries. I sing a song to her and sometimes she calms down.

Elizabeth, age 4½

Dear Elizabeth,
. . . You are learning so many things about being a big sister! One thing is that babies sometimes cry. It can be hard for everyone in the family when a baby cries.

Sometimes nothing helps to quiet the baby; at times like that, I wonder if babies just need to cry. At other times, babies cry to let people know they need something, and grown-ups can quiet them by giving them food or a clean diaper or a hug. Even big sisters can sometimes help by talking or singing to the baby, like you told me you do. Missy knows your voice from all the other voices in the world. Your voice is special to her, and it helps her know you care about her.

Elizabeth, when you're angry about your sister, you know there are things you can do that don't hurt her or you or anybody else. I wonder what helps you most at times like that?

Your new baby sister needs you for all kinds of times: happy times, sad times, lonely times. It can make a person feel really good to be needed. And that's what families are for—needing each other and caring about each other in all kinds of ways.

❀ Elizabeth's mother also wrote us a letter and added another common family concern:

Dear Mister Rogers,
Last week, on your program, Anna Platypus was
disappointed that Dr. Bill couldn't take her to the beach
because he had to work. Since my husband is a
physician, Elizabeth listened to this situation very closely
and afterwards was able to articulate some of her feelings
about those nights when Daddy works too late to see her
when he comes home.

Elizabeth's Mother

Dear Mrs. ———,
Nothing could please us more than to know that
something we talked about on our program helped
with some meaningful communication in your family.
That's why we named our company Family
Communications—because that's just what we hope
will happen from the materials we develop.

It's good to know that Elizabeth could talk with you
and her father about her feelings. I wonder what
feelings that conversation might have evoked in you
and your husband because I know that parents, too,
can have mixed feelings when their work keeps them
away from their children. When our children were
growing up, there certainly were difficult times for me
when I couldn't be there for them, when I felt they

really wanted me. There are no perfect parents who are always there . . . and I would venture a guess that through her talks with her parents about those times, Elizabeth is learning essential things about family relationships—that her feelings of disappointment or anger are natural and normal and that she can find healthy ways to cope with that kind of disappointment. Perhaps most importantly, she's learning that her mother and father care deeply about her, even when they can't be with her . . . and no matter what she's feeling.

Dear Mister Rogers,
My brother Michael is just starting to watch you with me. I am six years old, and he is three years old. He copies everything I do.

Katie, age 6

Dear Katie,
. . . I can understand there can be lots of feelings about a younger brother, and I wonder how you feel about the times when your brother copies what you

do. You might feel proud about that, but you might not like the way he copies you all the time.

Katie, copying what others do is one way children learn. You are important to your brother. That's why he wants to do the things you do. He wants to learn from you.

You might want to talk with your brother and with the grown-ups in your family about how you feel when he copies what you do. It often helps to talk about our feelings so that other people can know how we feel.

Dear Mister Rogers,
My name is Jessie. I watch you on T.V. everyday. Yesterday my mommy told me we are going to have twins in October. I wish that they were girls, but Mommy says they are both boys. I already have one brother, Joshua, and I really wanted a sister. I was very excited to have a new baby, but now I'm a little sad. I'm not sure I'm going to like having 3 brothers and no sisters! I thought if I wrote to you I'd feel a little better. You always make me feel special!

Jessie, age 4

Dear Jessie,

It meant a great deal to me that you wanted to let me know your feelings about the new babies that will be born into your family in October. You told me you were excited to have new babies in the family, but you're "a little sad" because your mother told you that the twins are boys, and you wanted a sister. I can understand that you wanted to have a sister, especially because you already have a brother. And it's good that you can talk about your feelings, even the difficult ones like feeling sad.

You told me your mother helped write your letter to me, and I think you are fortunate to have a mother who cares so much about you and about what you're feeling. You and she will be the "women" of your family. When the people we care about help us with disappointments in childhood, it can show us the way to work on the disappointments we might have later in our life.

When I was your age, I didn't have a sister or a brother. There were some lonely times for me. I even made up some pretend brothers and sisters. You might want to make up stories about having a sister, and you might want to draw pictures about what she might look like or what you and she might do together.

When your baby brothers are born and as they grow, you'll find some things about them that are very special for you. Of course in all families, there are many feelings. Some of them are happy feelings, and some aren't. I hope you will find some good things about being their big sister and helping them in very important ways as they grow. If you'd like to write to me after they're born, I'd be glad to hear from you again.

❀ Jessie wrote us another letter after her twin brothers were born, letting us know that things were going well. Here is an excerpt from our second letter to Jessie:

Dear Jessie,
It was wonderful to hear from you again. . . . It gave me a good feeling to know that what I wrote to you helped you feel better. I'm glad to know that you are finding some good things about brothers. Those babies surely have a very fine sister!

Dear Mister Rogers,
Please ask all kids to share toys with their brothers and
sisters.

Mahesh, age 4

Dear Mahesh,
. . . Sometimes it is easy to share. Sometimes it is hard
to share. It can help to know there are some
important things that a person shouldn't have to share
with anybody, things like a favorite stuffed animal or
toy or special blanket or pillow. I hope you and your
brothers and sisters talk about whatever is important
to you about sharing. Talking about your feelings can
often help.

Thank you for sharing your idea with me. That's
one fine way to be neighborly.

Dear Mister Rogers,
Since we've been learning about divorce, I have a
question of divorce. How are divorces begained?

Lynn, age 5

Dear Lynn,

. . . There can be many reasons that lead to people getting a divorce. Sometimes children worry that when their parents are upset, that might be the beginning of a divorce; but, Lynn, in all families there are angry and upsetting times as well as other times. Did you ever hear our song, "It's the people you like the most who can make you feel maddest"? The second part of that song says: "It's the people you like the most who can make you feel happiest."*

One time in the Neighborhood of Make-Believe, we pretended that Prince Tuesday was afraid that his parents were getting a divorce because he heard them arguing. He had just met a family that was divorced, and that's why he was worried about his own family getting a divorce. In fact, he was so upset that he wished he were a machine, because machines don't have feelings! His family and friends helped him talk about his worries, and he came to understand that angry feelings are natural in families, and he felt better when he saw that his parents were able to work through their problem.

Lynn, divorce is a grown-up matter, and if you have some questions about that, it can really help to talk

* See pages 18–19.

with the grown-ups in your family. They care about you and they care about your feelings. How fortunate you are to have a family that loves you so much!

❀ When we contacted Lynn's family for permission to use his question in this book, his parents told us that they were surprised by his question, too, because they were not divorced nor were they considering a separation. That made Lynn's question even more important because it confirmed once again for me the reason we decided to talk about divorce on *Mister Rogers' Neighborhood.*

When we first started our program in the late 1960s, I would never have imagined that we would talk about divorce on our television program. By the late 1970s, because divorce had become so widespread, worries about divorce were affecting children like Lynn, whose families were not even considering a separation. They had heard about it from other children or from adults around them talking about divorce, and it had turned into a real concern for them.

That's why we decided to make a full week of programs helping children know that while there are divorces in some families, arguments in families don't necessarily lead to a divorce. We also gave them a clear message that divorce is a grown-up problem, not caused by the children . . . and that no matter what their family was like, they have people who love them and who will take care of them.

I hope that Lynn's family realizes how healthy it is that they have been open to his question about how divorces are "begained." We have always believed that whatever is mentionable is much more manageable. When families help their children talk about whatever concerns them, they generally find that their children are better able to handle whatever they're worrying about or wondering.

Dear Mister Rogers,

I know that you have talked alot about divorce. My mom and dad are having trouble and are fighting alot. They want to split up for a few weeks. My stomach has been hurting because we have been talking about that. I feel a little sad, too, but I don't really know how I'm going to not miss them.

If you can think of any ideas, I would like you to send me back a letter and that would help me alot. I really hope you can help me.

I'm staying with my mom and brother when my daddy's going away. My dad is staying at my grandma and grandpa's house.

Carly, age 5½

Dear Carly,

Thank you for sending me a letter. It meant a lot to
me that you wanted to tell me some of your feelings
about the things that are happening in your family.
When parents want to separate and are thinking about
a divorce, there can be hard times for *everyone* in the
family. I hope that when you're having hard times and
feeling sad or angry or worried, you can talk about
whatever you're feeling with the grown-ups in your
family. In your letter you told me about some of your
feelings, and it's good that your mother wanted to help
you write to me. I'm glad that you are a person who
can talk about your feelings, and you are fortunate to
have a mother who cares so much about you and what
you're feeling.

We made some programs for *Mister Rogers'
Neighborhood* about divorce. They are repeated every
year, usually in the fall. I wonder if you saw any of
those. When we made those programs, we talked with
a lot of parents and children. One thing that seemed
to help the children was knowing the divorce was not
their fault. Separating and divorce are about grown-up
problems. Sometimes children worry about the bad
things they've done, and they think their behavior
made their parents want to get divorced. But, Carly, all

children do bad things once in a while. And, even in families where there's no divorce, there can be angry times.

It can also help to know that your parents still love you and that they will take good care of you, even if they don't live together. What gives me a good feeling about your letter, Carly, is sensing how much your family cares about you and about your feelings. Even though your mother and father may separate or get divorced, they will always be your parents, and they both love you. And you and your brother will always be their children. You obviously have a lot of love in your family, and I hope you can have good feelings about that.

❀ Carly wrote us another letter several months later:

Dear Mister Rogers,
My mom and dad are divorced now. I've been doing fine about it. I live with my mom most of the time. My brother is doing fine too. Now all my mom and dad fight about is when who should be with who.

Dear Carly,

It was wonderful to hear from you again. I remember when you wrote before, and it meant a lot to me that you wanted to let me know how things are going with your family.

You told me that your mother and father are divorced now. It's good to know you're feeling better about your family situation. Changes can be hard at first, and little by little, we often find that we can manage things that were hard for us at first. I'm glad it's been that way for you. I also think that you are fortunate to have a mother and father who care about you.

❀ Here is an excerpt from the letter we wrote to Carly's mother:

Dear Mrs. ———,

It was a pleasure to hear from your family again. I certainly do remember Carly's letter. She wrote so expressively about her concerns over the possibility of the divorce. I'm grateful to know that our answer last spring was meaningful for her.

It's very touching that Carly wanted to write again and tell us how she's doing. What a thoughtful girl she is! And how good it is to know that she has been able to deal with the changes that have come with the divorce! I believe that what helps children cope the best is the ongoing loving care from the people in their family who are close to them. The love she feels from you and from her father is surely important for her now and as she grows. To be sure, Carly and her brother are greatly blessed to have such a loving family.

Dear Mister Rogers,
I want to say Merry Christmas and Happy New Year to you. I am a little sad this Christmas, 'cause my Mommy and Daddy don't live together any more. They are angry at each other. But I know they are not angry at me and they love me. Even though my Daddy lives somewhere else, I see him a lot. He is helping me write this letter.
Alec, age 3, and his Daddy

Dear Alec,
Thank you for the beautiful card and your family's kind wishes for the holidays.

It meant a lot to me that you wanted to let me know your feelings about your parents' not living together. I wasn't surprised to know you are having some sad times about that. Children can have lots of feelings when their parents are divorced—some sad and even angry feelings. In your letter you told me about some of your feelings. It is good that you are a person who can talk about your feelings, especially the hard ones. I call that important talk.

You wanted me to know that even though your mother and father aren't living together, they are still your parents, and they both love you. I trust that you have very good feelings about that.

It can be hard to understand about love and angry feelings. In all families, along with the times that are loving and warm, there are times that are angry. All children do bad things once in a while, and their parents get angry with them. Sometimes, children are angry with their parents, too. I hope you know that loving people can get angry with each other once in a while—even in families where the mothers and fathers live together.

Alec, the people who loved you even before you were born—your mother and daddy—will always love you and give you the care that you need to grow in healthy ways. That's what it means to be PARENTS, whether they're divorced or not.

Dear Mr. Rogers,

My Grandma doesn't think very well anymore. She wears pull up diapers just like the ones I wore when I was getting potty trained, and she never knows who I am or my sister or even my Mommy. I like to play with her at the playground but sometimes it is really scary when she has a fit or when she runs away.

Sometimes Grandma says mean things and she makes me cry.

My big sister said that you are a Grandpa and that you think really good. How come my Grandma can't think like you?

I can sing the songs you sing, but sometimes I forget all of the words.

Nicole, age 3

Dear Nicole,

. . . You told me so many interesting things about yourself and your family. It's very hard for everyone in the family when a grandparent has a sickness like your grandmother has. It's hard to understand that your grandmother's problems come from a sickness in her mind. She might look fine on the outside and she may be very loving, but because of her sickness, she can't show her love in the way most people do. I was sorry to know that sometimes you are scared by some of the things your grandmother does and that sometimes she makes you cry. How hard that must be for you! Even when you love someone, you can still have times when you feel angry or scared or sad about that person. In fact, it's so natural to feel two ways about the same person or thing that there's even a word for that feeling. That word is "ambivalent."

You and your family might like to know that there are children's books about other children whose grandparents have that kind of sickness. Maybe a librarian can help your family find some. When people read about things in a book, things that they're going through, it can be comforting to know others are living through times like that, too.

It also helps to talk about your feelings about your grandmother, and I'm glad you could share some of your feelings in your letter to me. The people in your family care about your feelings, too. Even though your grandmother cannot show you her love in the way that you would like, I hope you know that your love for her will always be a part of her life, and her love for you will always be a part of yours. No sickness can take away all that you and your grandma have meant to each other.

Nicole, I'm glad to know you like our television visits and our songs. You told me you forget some of the words. I hope you understand that when you forget something, that's a different kind of forgetting than the sickness your grandmother has. Everybody forgets things once in a while.

❀ Another warm family story came to us from a young woman:

Dear Mister Rogers,
(A long time ago) I sent a letter to you penned by my older sister Becky. It went something like:

Dear Mister Rogers,
My name is Caroline. I am 5 years old. My favorite color is blue. I really like your show and Daniel Striped Tiger.

I was very pleased when a reply came from you and a picture of yourself. You said that you were very glad that I liked your show and the next time you wore your blue

*sweater, you would think of me. Well, that was in 1971
and we didn't have a color television. I cried until it
must have looked as though my heart were going to
break, but my dad came up with a solution. Every night
after work for about a week, he would walk me to the
furniture store and we would sit in a recliner chair and
watch your show. When you finally wore your blue
sweater, I was thrilled, but then I watched at home in
black and white. It was a very nice time for my dad and
I—he worked hard, so quiet time was rare. It's a nice
memory of a younger time to take to adulthood or one
day my own children.*

❀ Here's an excerpt from our answer to her:

Dear Caroline,

. . . That was such a wonderful story you shared with
us about the letter you sent us when you were five
years old. It was an important reminder to us that we
never know how our communication will be received!
What I had intended as a kind thought had,
unfortunately, turned into a difficult disappointment! I
was so impressed by the caring way your father helped

you turn your heartbreak into a treasured experience
—by being resourceful in finding a way to help you
see a color television set at the furniture store. How
fortunate you are to have such a caring father!

❀ Kindness and thoughfulness are things we "catch" from
experiences with our parents and with others who are close
to us. This woman's letter is a wonderful confirmation of
how likely we are to incorporate warm family memories into
our lives. They become part of what we want to then pass
on to children, through our families and through our work.

Since people in families care so deeply about one another,
family joys can be great and family tensions can be intense.
We often hear such things in the mail we receive.

That's why I feel it's especially important to help children
understand that family life can have a mix of love and anger,
pride and disappointment, kindness and intolerance. We encourage children to put their feelings into words. When the
adults they love can listen and respond in love, that's real
communication. Early family communication is the bedrock
in which all future communication is built.

CHAPTER EIGHT

Today my
dog died

Dear Mr. Rogers,
Today My Dog Died.
I was very sad. He
will always be in are
Hearts. This afternoon we
Had a little funeral.

Love,
Avital

6/3/88

(Avital, age 7)

Dear Mister Rogers,
My dog Max died. It still makes me feel sad.
Michael, age 3

Dear Michael,
It meant a lot to me that you wanted to send me a letter and let me know about Max. I was sorry to know that he died, and I can understand it still makes you feel sad. When I was a boy, my dog Mitzie died, and that was a hard time for me.

People can have lots of difficult feelings when a pet dies. No matter how sad you feel now, you probably won't always feel that way. After a while, when your sadness has gone away, you'll be able to feel happy again about the good times you and your pet had together.

It can help to talk about your feelings, and that's why it's good that you wanted to talk about your sadness in your letter to me. Your family cares about your feelings, too, and I hope you can talk about whatever you're feeling with the grown-ups in your family. I have always called that "important talk."

Our cat Sybil died a while ago, and I still miss her. It helps to have pictures of her and to think about the memories of her being on my lap or sitting nearby at breakfast. Sometimes it helps to talk about her, and sometimes it helps just to be alone and quiet. I wonder what helps you? Happy times and sad times are part of everyone's life, but you can grow to know that the love you and Max shared is still alive in you and always will be.

❀ It has meant a great deal to me that children and families feel they can trust me with some very deep feelings about such a thing as the death of their beloved family pet. For many children, that is their first experience with death. It's a beginning step in confronting one of the hard facts of life—that all living things eventually die.

Some well-meaning people have said to their children, "Don't be sad, we'll get you another pet," but it's obvious even from the letters we've received that children need to express their painful feelings. It helps them to say that they're sad, and they need time to grieve.

Children grieve, just as we do, when we've suffered a loss. We can also help them know that we're sad when we are and that the heavy sadness won't be forever . . . and it can often help to turn to others for comfort. Helping children deal with their feelings when a pet dies tills the soil for other hard losses they'll deal with later on in life.

Many people have written to us about their four- or five-year-olds asking questions about death. At that age, children are curious about something they can't see or touch. They're trying to make sense of this thing adults call "death." They're trying to figure it out.

Beyond that, they have natural fears of being separated from the ones they love. What an important time for them to be concerned about that, just when they're wanting to be independent and grown up! They know, at the same time, that they're still very much dependent on the grown-ups they love.

It's no wonder those questions make us feel uncomfortable. It's scary for us, too, to think about not being with them or the others who mean the most to us. We can reassure them that we, too, hope to be with them for a long, long time.

Dear Mister Rogers,
I have a three-and-a-half-year-old son, Neil . . . Neil is
fortunate to have both sets of grandparents who adore
him, and he is also their first grandchild. He loves to
spend time with them. Recently, he has been asking me
questions about my grandparents and where they were. I
told him about the wonderful time I had with them and
that they had died and gone to heaven. Neil has later
told me that he would like to go and get them back
for me.

Olina, Neil's mother

Dear Mrs. ———,
Thank you for letting me know about Neil's
relationship with his grandparents. My grandparents
were close to me, too, when I was growing up, and
now my wife and I are grandparents to our young
grandsons. I know what that special relationship can
mean—on both sides.

You also told us about Neil's concerns for your
grandparents who have died. How touching it was to
hear that he wanted to go to Heaven to get them back
for you! That could well be his way of letting you
know how much his grandparents mean to him.

It is difficult to help children with such things as death and Heaven. Chidren, like most of us, can understand more easily what they see and touch and get to know in a direct, hands-on way. Children have such a difficult time understanding that death is final. In a simple conversation like that, it may help children to hear once again that when people have died, even though we miss them, they can't come back. That's just the way death is.

It's often hard for parents to know how to react at times like that—how much to say and how much not to say. I've found that it's usually best to say something simple and short and then to leave the door open so children can feel comfortable coming to us again if they want more.

The best thing that happens in such conversations is that children discover that they can talk about anything with us. And when we show children that we adults can talk about our feelings when someone has died, we're letting them know that there are sad times in everyone's life, and that we can manage even the most painful feelings, especially when we talk about them with people who care about us.

Neil is certainly fortunate to have a mother like you

who wants to help him understand difficult and
sensitive things. Just your wanting to help him can be
most important of all.

Dear Mister Rogers,
A few days ago, our 4¾-year-old daughter had trouble
going to sleep. She seemed troubled by something and
was rubbing her eyes as if she was crying. I asked her if
she wanted to talk to me about anything. She said "no."
Several minutes later when she was in bed and I was
with her, she began to have quite a fit and said the
following, "I don't want to die. I don't want to get older.
I want to be a baby again. I don't want to be in a box
all by myself under the ground. If I die, I want to be
with everyone in our family in a box under the ground."

Ken

Dear Mr. ———,
We can well understand your frustration in helping
your child deal with her worries, but we also hope you
will know that your daughter's fears about death are
quite natural at her age. Of course, the thought of

being separated from loved ones is threatening, no matter how old we are.

As with most things in parenthood, there are no easy answers. In general, though, it can help children to know that they are not alone in their fears about death, that most children—and even adults—think about that. At the same time, it can also help to let them know that we expect that they'll be living a long, long time. And, in fact, we can tell them honestly that most people do live to be very old. However, these aren't magic answers. Fears generally take a long time to be resolved. What seems to help the most is for children to hear hope and love and reassurance in their parents' voices.

You may be interested to know that we have long believed that whatever is mentionable can be much more manageable. And what I applaud most about your letter is that your daughter felt she could confide in you, even about her scariest thoughts. Your loving care is obvious in your letter, and it certainly must be a solace to your daughter. That kind of care will continue to nourish her as she grows. She obviously wants you to be there growing along with her for a long, long time!

Dear Mister Rogers,
My grandpa died. It has been very [hard] for me to take.
His name is Kenith. His funeral was Friday the third. I
watched your show. It was about a ballet class. I am in
ballet.

Lauren, age 8

Dear Lauren,
Thank you for sending me a letter. I'm glad to know
you like our television visits and that you especially
liked the one where we went to a ballet class. It takes a
lot of practice to be able to do ballet dancing well. I'm
proud of you for all the work you're doing for your
ballet dancing.

Lauren, it meant a lot to me that you wanted to tell
me your grandfather died. Your grandfather obviously
meant a great deal to you, and I'm sorry to know that
he died. You wrote that his death was very hard for
you, and I can understand that. I was close to my
grandparents, too, and it was hard for me when they
died. When someone you care about has died, there
can be many difficult feelings.

It's good that you can let people know when things
are hard for you. I hope you know there are many
people who care about you and about your feelings.

You are a special person, Lauren, and I can imagine how your grandfather must have really appreciated your love. He will always be an important part of your life: the love you shared with him will always be alive in you.

❀ What struck me about Lauren's letter is how she offered both sides of herself: she at first expressed her sadness about her grandpa and then moved right on to talk about our program and her ballet lessons. Life goes on, even in the midst of sadness.

Dear Mister Rogers,
My husband died suddenly recently. . . . My 4-year-old granddaughter, Heather, believes that when you come on the air that you are talking to her personally, and she talks back to the television set as though you can hear her as well. Recently you were singing a song about feelings and were encouraging the children to talk about them with someone. From the other room, I heard her saying to the television set, "I have feelings, Mister Rogers. I'm sad, Mister Rogers." Just then you said it's okay to be angry and to tell someone about it. So Heather said, "I am! I'm angry, too! I'm sad and even

Grandma said it's okay to be angry." She continued to
pour out her little heart to you. . . . I held her in my
arms and we both wept.

Heather's Grandma

Dear Mrs. ————,

. . . We're especially grateful for your beautiful story
about Heather's reaction to one of our programs.
While we're honored to know you appreciated that we
helped her share her feelings that day, at the same
time we are very much aware that the children who
seem to use our Neighborhood best are the ones who
have already experienced the deep investment of their
own families in their development, and thus are able
to understand what we offer. I certainly heard that
confirmed in your letter, and I couldn't help but think
how fortunate your granddaughter is to have such a
loving grandmother. I can be only a television friend;
how important that you were there for her at that
time when she obviously needed you.

The losses Heather has faced are your losses as well,
and I hope that you have caring support around you
for your needs. Our hearts and our prayers are with
you, and we will remember with great pleasure that
you and Heather are a part of our Neighborhood.

Dear Mister Rogers,
Matthew's grandma passed away after 3 months of
illness. Matthew faithfully said prayers for his "Ga-Ga"
(grandma) every night. Perhaps he missed a few, because
when learning of Ga-Ga's death, he immediately went
into tears and said it was his fault for not praying.

Matthew's mother

Dear Mrs. ———,

. . . You were particularly worried that your child's
faith in prayer may have been shattered. At five years
of age, a child's sense of prayer is largely magical; it is
a way of getting things or making something happen.
When that didn't work, your son naturally lost faith in
that definition of prayer. But prayer means different
things to different people at different times in their
lives. As he grows and has more experiences in life, he
will probably come to new and more mature
definitions of prayer and will form his own ideas about
what it means to him. Most people—adults and
children—who have lost a loved one often feel guilty,
helpless, and angry. That's only natural. Even if we
have a sense that the person who died is in the loving
hands of God, there still can be painful and angry
feelings because we miss that person. Letting your

child know that his feelings are natural may be one of the most helpful things you can do. Whatever your feelings may be at this time are natural, too. Please know that our thoughts are with you and your whole family.

Dear Mister Rogers,
Did you know that our baby died? I feel sad that it died.
It was in my mommy's tummy when our baby died. I'm
almost four.

Erica, age 3

❀ Erica's mother wrote us a letter as well:

Dear Mister Rogers,
About a month ago, when I was two and a half months
pregnant, I had a miscarriage. It was hard for all of us,
but I have been especially surprised by how it seems to
have affected my almost four-year-old daughter Erica.
She asked the other day to write to you about it. . . . She

seems especially concerned that when she grows up her babies may die too, and often wonders why the baby died.

Erica's Mom

Dear Erica,

. . . It meant so much to me that you wanted to tell me that the baby died. I was very sorry to know that. I can understand that you feel sad about the baby dying, and it's good that you can talk about your feelings. Children can have lots of different feelings when a sister or brother has died, even some hard feelings, like sad and angry. I hope you can talk about whatever you're feeling with the grown-ups in your family. I have always called that important talk, and you are fortunate to have a family that cares about what you're feeling.

Sometimes children worry that they may have made bad things happen because they thought something or did something bad. But all children do bad things and think bad things now and then. Doing something bad or good, or thinking and wishing bad or good things don't make things happen—not good things or bad things. That reminds me of our song "Wishes Don't Make Things Come True."

Wishes Don't Make Things Come True

One time I wished that a lion would come
And eat up my house and my street.
I was mad at the world and I wished that the
   beast
Would stomp everything with his big, heavy feet
And eat everything with his big, sharp teeth,
And eat everything with his teeth.

But that wish certainly didn't come true
'Cause scary, mad wishes don't make things come
   true.

One time I wished that a dragon would come
And burn up my daddy's big store.
I was angry with him 'cause I wanted to play,
But my daddy just went to his store right away.
I wished that the dragon would burn his store.
I wished it would burn daddy's store.

But that wish certainly didn't come true
'Cause scary, mad wishes don't make things come
   true.

Everyone wishes for scary, mad things.
I'd guess that you sometimes do, too.
I've wished for so many
And I can say
That all kinds of wishes
Are things just like play.
They're things
That our thinking has made—
So wish then
And don't be afraid.
I'm glad it's certainly that way, aren't you?
That scary, mad wishes don't make things come
  true.
No kinds of wishes can make things come true.

Erica, it can be hard—for grown-ups and children
—to understand how a baby gets born or how a baby
dies. As you grow, little by little you'll find more ways
to think about things like that. For now, it's good that
you can talk with your mom and dad about whatever
you're thinking or feeling.

❀ Here is an excerpt from the letter we sent to Erica's
mother:

Dear Mrs. ————,

We were very touched by Erica's letter. And we appreciated that you wanted to write and help us know more about your family and the circumstances around the baby's death.

Children have their own ways of grieving, some ways like ours and some ways different. I can understand that you were surprised by Erica's reactions, even now a month later. You might be interested to know that we recently heard from another family that had experienced a miscarriage and had a preschooler with similar concerns.

Children can have a difficult time with a miscarriage, because they have formed a relationship in their minds with a little brother or sister, from the time they first hear about the new baby. So even though it may seem as if the grief should be easier for children to handle—easier than if they knew the baby —that experience can be as complicated and painful as any other death because the children have lost the relationship they've formed in their mind. And so have you and your husband. I hope you and he have good support from family and friends for your own feelings.

We trust that you can appreciate that the best help

you can give your daughter is your openness to her concerns and her feelings and her questions. From what you told us and from Erica's letter, it is obvious that you are already helping her in that way. It seems like you've established a "safe" atmosphere for your daughter over the years. Erica is fortunate to be growing up in a home where she knows her parents care about her deepest worries.

❀ Another letter with a similar concern came from a minister who wrote to tell us about a family in her church who was dealing with a stillborn baby.

Dear Mister Rogers,
The three year old in the family is having real problems dealing with it—[she's saying,] "I must have been bad . . . I promise to be good if we can have a baby."

❀ Also, through a telephone call that came to our office, we got to know another family dealing with the tragic and unexpected death of their two-year-old daughter. In the course of her conversation, the mother told us that her eight-year-old daughter, Jennifer, was especially concerned about something she had said to her little sister. Earlier in the week, Abigail, being a typical toddler, wandered into Jennifer's room and messed up some of her papers and treasures. With the furor and frustration that's certainly understandable from an older sister in that situation, Jennifer sent the toddler out of her room, saying, "Don't come back!"

I hope that mother can appreciate what an important gift she gave Jennifer over the years—the gift of knowing she could approach her with her most painful thoughts and her deepest fears. Had Jennifer not confided in her mother about her angry words with her sister, it's quite possible that she might have held inside her for years the deep, dark worry that she may have somehow been responsible for the family's tragedy. It's also quite possible that her guilt might have been devastating.

In our letter to Jennifer we included our comments about the song "Wishes Don't Make Things Come True."* A few weeks later, the family sent us a book that Jennifer wrote to help other children dealing with the death of a sister or brother. The page of her book that follows is strong testimony to how important it was to her to know that she didn't cause her sister's death with her "scary mad" wishes.

* See page 140.

Some children, after somebody they love dies, they recall the times they told that person "Go away" or "I hope I never see you again." I want those children to understand that scary mad wishes don't make things come true. Some children feel guilty. I want them to understand that they didn't do anything to make that person die.

Jennifer

❈ Throughout their lives, children will find themselves dealing with death. It's not our constant smiling that will help them feel secure. Rather, it's their knowing that love can hold many feelings, including sadness, and that they can trust that there will always be people who love them and who will care about them through all kinds of times—the painfully sad times as well as the joyful times.

CHAPTER NINE

Whys

Dear Mr. Rogers

Lynsie is A 4 year old who just Loves your show! She says she learns so much from you. As parents we Are so thankful for you! Lynsie would Love A letter or picture from you. She wants to be AN Architect And go to Carnegie Mellon Like her Dad.

(Lynsie, age 4)

Dear Mister Rogers,

*I have a 2½-year-old daughter. . . . As you know, from
the time children can talk—and before—they are
incredibly curious. That results in a string of "whys"
that, while I enjoy the challenge of it and the sheer joy
she gets from learning, can wear me down after a few
hours! She's learned that a "why" that she really wants
answered almost always gets a response, but sometimes
when she plays the "why game," Mom reserves the right
not to play for a while. The "why game" is a series of
"whys" designed to prolong interaction, not really to get
information. So I try to answer, "You really seem to
want to talk about this!" And if I just can't take the
time, or if I don't have the mental energy, I tell
her so.*

*She and I have made up short songs about WHY—
whys are great, they help us learn, sometimes they make
mommy impatient, etc. . . . I was wondering if you've*

*ever done a show on WHY, or if you've done songs
on WHY.*

*I would really enjoy learning or seeing anything
you've done on the subject.*

Kathryn

Dear Mrs. ———,

It's certainly understandable that as a sensitive and
caring mother, you are trying to find healthy ways to
deal with your daughter's "whys" because they can be
incessant! It's good that you're trying to understand
what's underneath your daughter's questioning. There
is much to appreciate about children's "whys." Young
children generally start asking a lot of "whys" after
they've mastered language. Now they can go beyond
just naming things: they can use words to gather
information, and they're amazed that adults know lots
of things.

About that same time, young children are just
beginning to consider cause and effect relationships in
the world. They can be insatiably curious about how
the world operates. On top of all that, what's just been
learned tends to be used by children over and over, as

if they were driven to repeat it in order to make it a permanent part of themselves.

As with most things in parenthood, there are no easy answers. Parents have to trust their instincts and try to think of the children's needs as well as their own needs. That's what makes parenthood such a challenge. I appreciated reading about the warm ways you've responded to your daughter, ways that allow her to know you respect her asking and her thirst for information.

You asked if we've discussed "whys" on our program or sung about that. In fact, we do have a song called "Some Things I Don't Understand" that is about "why." We're happy to enclose it for you. And, we'll be glad to keep your letter in our suggestion file which we refer to when we plan our new programs. It helps us in many ways to hear from friends like you.

SOME THINGS I DON'T UNDERSTAND

Some things I don't understand.
Some things are scary and sad.
Sometimes I even get bad when I'm mad.
Sometimes I even get glad.

Why does a dog have to bark?
Why does an elephant die?
Why can't we play all the time in the park?
Why can't my pussycat fly?

Why, why, why, why, why, why?
I wonder why.
Why, why, why, why, why, why?
I wonder why.

Why do big people say "No"?
Why are their voices so loud?
Why don't the witches and bad guys all go?
Why does the sky fly a cloud?

(Chorus)

Why does it have to get dark?
Why can't the day always stay?
Let's say goodbye to the night time, Goodbye.
Let's send the dark time away.

Some day, oh some day, I'll know what to say.
Some day, oh some day, I'll not have to say

Why? Why? Why? . . .

Dear Mister Rogers,

Sebastien—who is almost six—and I are writing to you to find out if you would consider talking, during one of your television visits, about games and whether it is important to learn how to play games with friends.

Sebastien does not enjoy playing games in which anyone wins and therefore someone else loses. He prefers to play by himself rather than to play any games like that. This is fine at times, but it means that at camp, at school, and at birthday parties he does not participate in many of the activities with the other children.

We've been talking about how playing games is just one way of doing things with other people, and that doing things with other people is a way of sharing and caring. We've also talked about how winning and losing are not as important as just playing and having fun during a game. But I know that's a difficult concept to accept. Adults have a hard time with it themselves. Thanks for listening.

Sebastien and his mother

Dear Mrs. ———,

. . . You and Sebastien certainly aren't alone in your struggles with this! Many children have trouble with competition and games, and many parents worry about how to deal with their children's feelings about winning and losing.

As with most things that trouble parents, there are no easy answers, and if "competition" continues to be a problem, you may want to consider looking for someone like a teacher or counselor in your area to talk with about that. You may also find that being uncomfortable with competition is part of Sebastien's basic nature, and he may continue all his life to seek other directions than those which lead him into situations that are clearly competitive. I've always believed that, for the most part, parents know their children best and can trust their instincts about what is helpful to pursue and what isn't. From the ways you describe how you've been helping Sebastien, it's obvious that you are offering a great deal of thoughtful and loving care to your son. How fortunate he is to have a mother like you!

Dear Sebastien,

You and your mother wanted to send me a letter telling me your feelings about games. I can understand that you don't like certain games. Playing games can be difficult for a lot of children. What was important to me about your letter is that you and your mother are talking about your feelings and the feelings that people have about winning and losing. I've always believed that talking about feelings is "important talk." And you are fortunate to have a mother and other people in your life who care so much about you and your feelings.

Dear Mister Rogers,
I know that it is normal for children to have lots of play about guns, battles, killing, etc. The only "normal" sized guns my husband and I have allowed in the house are waterguns, and they're not terribly realistic looking—one is made from red plastic, the other pink.

We have two sons (Ben is 6, Sam is 3½). So much of their play seems to be around this theme of good guys/ bad guys, shooting, and killing. They watch almost no commercial TV, so I don't quite get where this comes from. Thankfully, it isn't the only way they play—I'd go crazy if it was. But it is a dominant theme. My sense is that if I try to squash it, it will come out other ways. Anyway, I really wouldn't want to do that. I guess I'm not even sure what I'm asking. There just seems to be so much violence in the world around us that I was hoping

I would be able to keep it from them. Perhaps that is
unrealistic, and maybe I just need to keep this in
perspective. Any comments?

Mary Lou

Dear Mrs. —————,

It means a great deal to us that you turned to us for
help with your concern about children and gun play.
As you can well imagine, that's a dilemma for many
parents, and we can understand how disturbing it is to
deal with. . . .

❀ Along with our letter, we also sent the following excerpts
from some of our writings:

Parents often find, to their dismay, that, at a certain
age, young children turn almost everything they pick
up into a "gun," and that if there isn't anything to
pick up, a cocked thumb and forefinger do just as
well. "Bang! Bang!" or "Gotcha!" resound both
indoors and out, and one dramatic death scene after
another takes place on the living room rug or in the
shrubbery.

There are many reasons that "violent play" of this

kind becomes so compelling for children. That they
need to feel powerful and in control is certainly a big
one. The person with the gun literally "calls the shots."
If a child has cooperative playmates, they may act
afraid of the gunslinger. They may even let themselves
be ordered around, or fall down and lie still when
they're "shot."

Guns seem to confer a kind of super power because
they can make things happen at a distance, as though
a person's arms were enormously long. Perhaps for
this same reason, remote control toys like train sets or
battery-driven cars often have a powerful attraction for
young children. Certainly water pistols confer "power,"
and many of us can remember how hard it was not to
squirt someone with the garden hose when we were
meant to be watering the flowers or washing the car.
Even flashlights have this power and are reassuring to
children who are afraid of the dark.

Almost anything that extends our control over the
world around us is bound to have a strong lure for us
all our lives. In itself, that urge is a tremendous
motivation for creativity and invention, for learning
how to control disease or for finding ways to make
deserts bloom. But, of course, it's also the same urge
that leads some people to find ways to control others

through fear of physical harm or death. How to make this urge a constructive force in our children's lives is a problem all adults face. Certainly television and comics and real-life events all seem to conspire against us by emphasizing negative models of people who want to be in control through violent acts. Again and again we learn from killers or would-be assassins in the news that their motivation was, at least in part, the desire "to show the world that I'm not just a nobody."

I don't think many of us believe that when our children play with pretend guns it means that they are likely to grow up to use real ones. But, even so, that form of play can be very painful to us because it touches our own deep feelings about death, loss, love, and the value of human life. *Those of us who are made uncomfortable by gun play need to let our children know it and let them know in as many ways as we know how that they are valuable to us.* Even though we can never stop our children from engaging in some form of gun play when they are out of our sight, we can certainly refuse to buy realistic-looking gun toys for them; and, as one family I know did, we can have a firm rule against gun play in the house. In that family, all guns of any kind were "checked at the front door." We can also discuss with our children the use of guns and other forms of violence that they see in comics or on television.

What is important is not so much whether our children engage in gun play, but whether they know how we feel about it—or about anything else they do. Our children need us to be able to make rules that express our values and help ensure their safety. Children may sometimes find the reasons for these rules hard to understand or may consider the rules unreasonable. "But Johnny's parents let him stay up till ten" is something we may hear; I think the answer is a simple one that children, in their own way, can comprehend: "But you're not growing up in Johnny's family, and we feel differently about it." It is from the people they love the most that children acquire most of their long-term values.

Dear Mister Rogers,
This time I am writing to you for advice. I respect you so much and I feel that you have a sensitivity towards a child's feelings. When my son Shaun was 2, I took him to a "Mommy and Me" program—a 1 hour nursery

school atmosphere where the mothers would stay in the room. He loved it and made many friends whom we still see today.

After that year, I enrolled him in a nursery school program with the same teacher, assuming that her familiar face would be a help in the transition from "Mommy and Me" to where he would be on his own for two hrs. twice a week. On the first day he was excited about going and cheerfully went into the building. I didn't give it another thought and went about my errands.

However, when I picked him up, he was a pitiful sight. He was standing at the bottom of the stairs crying his eyes out. When I asked the teachers what the problem was, they said he just started crying at 10:00 A.M. and called for me. Personally, I think that they had overbooked the first day (22 kids instead of 14) and he felt lost in the shuffle and was severely frightened. When I ask him what happened, he just says that he's not going to school. I tried taking him back the next week, but he wouldn't let go of my hand for a second. Ever since that time, when someone mentions school, he freezes and gets so upset that it is upsetting to me.

I thought that perhaps if I let it slide for a while he would forget (he didn't), and lately I've tried talking to *him about it (it infuriates him, he cries hysterically and begs me not to make him go). Kindergarten will begin soon and I don't know what to do.*

I have spoken to many people concerning this problem, including his doctor, with no real satisfaction. Most say that he'll just have to cry it out and get over it. Perhaps I'm too sensitive to the problem, but I don't think that is the thing to do. He becomes practically hysterical when I just talk about it. What can I do— drag him to school? His best friend, Matthew, will also be starting school, and I have requested that they are in the same session, figuring that he might give him moral support.

It's only because I trust you so much—you really do care about children—that I felt compelled to write to you at this time.

Kimberly

Dear Mrs. ———,

It meant a great deal to know you trusted me with your concerns about Shaun's attitude toward school. Your sensitivity to his needs must be very important to him. As I read your letter, I thought about how fortunate he is to have a mother like you who cares deeply about what troubles him.

There may be many reasons why a certain child may have problems with separation when it is time to go to school. And that is also why there are different ways to help different children when they are concerned about that. I suppose the advice you have been given of "letting him cry it out" is based on the experience that most children will stop crying after a reasonable period of time and will adjust to the new experience. That may be because the crying can be an expression of demanding to be in control, or a way to seek attention, or a reflection of a parent's reluctance to have his or her child move into a more independent situation. But for other children, the crying may mean that that child needs more time to adjust. For such children, it can help to have the parent stay in the kindergarten classroom for a while—if need be even for several weeks—until the child begins to trust the teacher and "school."

The more I work with children, the more humble I feel about giving specific advice. You are the one who knows your child best. Maybe in talking through your feelings about the situation with the people at your son's school, you may be able to come to some resolution that you will be comfortable with. Sometimes it can be very difficult to ask for exceptions to the rules when the school system seems to be geared for group norms and not individuals. I certainly empathize with your struggles to do what is best for Shaun. I wonder if you've ever talked with him about *your* first days of school—truthfully telling him how you felt about them. Is he able to understand that you were little once, too?

✿ A number of years ago, we received a touching letter from a mother who was trying to find creative ways to help her son feel more comfortable with his prescribed eye patch. Eye patches and eyeglasses are somewhat common for young children, and helping a child to become accustomed to his or her new eye patch or pair of eyeglasses takes a caring medical team and patient parents. In this particular letter, Justin's mother wrote to tell us that her son's physician had just suggested that her Justin wear arm braces to keep him from taking off his eye patch.

Dear Mrs. ———,
. . . We hope you can appreciate that there are no magic answers for help with such a difficult experience for a young child as wearing an eye patch and glasses.

Eye patches and arm braces can be very scary and
confining because young children are so dependent on
their eyes and their hands in order to experience the
world. I remember a mother who wrote to us long ago
whose son refused to use his eye patch, and she told
us that one day *she* tried on an eye patch and found it
to be terribly upsetting for her. That firsthand
experience helped her realize why it was so hard for
her son—and gave her new energy to find some
comforting ways of helping him very gradually get
used to wearing the patch.

We wondered if you may be able to talk with other
parents who have young children who have had to
deal with the concerns you and Justin have. Would
there be someone on the medical team, such as a
social worker or pediatric nurse, whom you would feel
comfortable talking with and who might have
experience with young children's feelings about
their disabilities or eye problems? Perhaps there may
be a child development specialist in your area who
could get to know you and Justin and could support
you in finding good ways of helping Justin to
cope.

Thank you for being in touch with us. Our hearts

are with you and Justin. We will remember with pleasure that your family is watching our Neighborhood.

Dear Justin,

It was good to get to know you from your mother's letter. I'm glad that you enjoy our television visits.

Your mother told me about your eye patch and eyeglasses, and I can understand that they are hard for children to wear. Sometimes we talk about eye patches and eyeglasses on our television visits.

There can be lots of angry feelings, especially at first, when children have to wear things like patches and glasses, and I hope when you feel that way, you can *say* that you're angry and that you can find healthy things to do with the mad that you feel. That's like our song, "What Do You Do with the Mad That You Feel?" I wonder what helps you when you're feeling angry?

Justin, it's good to know that we're television friends. You are special—just because you're you.

❀ We were happy to hear from Justin's mother again a little while later:

Dear Mister Rogers,
As you suggested, I've been trying to talk to other parents
with children who need glasses and an eye patch. I've
met one boy, who wears his glasses, but his mother can't
get him to wear the patch. I guess I'm not alone in this.

❀ Just knowing we aren't alone can give us added strength
to keep on searching for better and better solutions to our
challenges. The longer we live, the more we can realize that
everybody has at least one challenge if not many!

Dear Mister Rogers,
For the past five years I have been performing as Santa
Claus during the Christmas season. It is, indeed, a joyous
and warm experience. The more I do it, however, the
more impressed I become with how sensitive a process
this is and how important it is that I bring to it the kind
of gentleness, love and understanding you manifest as
Mr. Rogers. It is time, I think, for a more up-to-date
Santa Claus. One that is not a bribing, threatening,
overpowering figure.

It would be helpful to me as I try to develop my
Santa character to receive your own view of who Santa is

*and what he should try to be to children. What kinds of
things should Santa say or be sure not to say?*

*I would indeed be grateful if you could address
yourself to my concerns.*

Armando

Dear Mr. —————,

We appreciated that you wanted to be in touch with
us as you think about how you can present a helpful
image of Santa Claus for children. We have some
writings about Santa Claus and the holidays that we're
glad to share with you. We also wondered if you
might want to talk about your concerns with a
professor of Child Development or with some
preschool teachers in your area. We've always believed
the best help in our own creative growth comes
through caring and ongoing relationships, and we hope
you can find people like that in your area.

You've already made the best start, which is *wanting*
to present yourself to the children in a meaningful
way. You're obviously a thoughtful man. We hope
things will go well for you and the children you care
about.

❀ Here is an excerpt from our writings that we sent:

You may have noticed how frightened a small child can be at the sight of a department-store Santa Claus. There are so many stories and so much lore that our culture has built up around the figure of Santa Claus. How he became a symbol for rewarding "good" children and punishing "bad" children no one seems to be completely sure, but he certainly touches children and families very widely and deeply. Part of the Santa lore is that he spies on you when you're asleep and knows when you're being bad or good, and I don't think that's helpful for children, whose feelings about Santa are rooted in their view of their parents' omnipotence. It can only reinforce a fear that there *are* adults who see all, hear all, and know all.

Children listen with literal minds. Words have not yet taken on those abstract connotations they have for adults. So when a child hears, "He sees you when you're sleeping. . . . He knows when you've been bad or good!" the child may really believe it is so.

A healthy child grows up with the sense of being a whole person—a unique person separate and distinct from any other, with an inner privacy that can be shared or not shared as he or she sees fit. There is no one on this earth who sees all, hears all, and knows all about any one of us. Who we are inside and what we

do alone is our business. What we choose to tell and
to whom we choose to tell it is our business, too.

Here's how we handled children's concerns about
Santa Claus on our program:

In the Neighborhood of Make-Believe there is
general excitement because Betty Aberlin brings the
news that Santa is going to pay the neighbors a visit.
One neighbor, the puppet Daniel Striped Tiger, isn't
excited at all. He's plain scared.

"What's he going to do to us?" he asks.

Betty replies that it will probably be something nice,
but Daniel isn't reassured at all. "I try to be good, but
I'm not always good," he says. "I think I'm afraid of
Santa Claus. I wish he weren't coming here."

Betty Aberlin is surprised until Daniel explains that
he has heard that Santa sees you when you're sleeping
and knows when you're good and bad. She suggests to
Daniel that he talk with Santa about that when he
comes. It's a scary prospect for Daniel, but he agrees
to try.

When Santa stops by the clock where Daniel lives,
the first thing Daniel blurts out is, "Oh, my! You did
come! I'm Daniel Striped Tiger, and I'm not always
good!"

To which Santa replies, "Well, I'm Santa Claus, and I'm not always good either." And he adds, "Good people aren't always good. They just *try* to be."

As Santa is about to leave, Daniel gathers up his courage to pose the big question that's been on his mind.

"Can you see people when they're sleeping, and do you know when everybody's bad or good?" he asks.

"Of course not," says Santa. "Somebody made that up about me. I'm not a spy, and I can't see people when they're asleep."

"You can't?" asks Daniel.

"Of course not," Santa replies, "and I know that everybody's good sometimes and everybody's bad sometimes."

Daniel tells Santa that he's decided he likes him after all.

"I like you, too," says Santa, "and I'm glad you asked me that."

Every person, young and old, needs to keep a sense of privacy within, to know that his innermost good feelings and mad wishes, happy thoughts and bad dreams, can be kept all to himself or shared just as he wants.

Dear Mister Rogers,
I like playing with my Mom's friend's piano—how old do you think I should be before I start learning how to play?

Gregory, age 5, and his Mom

Dear Gregory,
You told me you like playing with your mom's friend's piano. "Playing with" a piano is a good way to begin learning about it. You asked how old should you be before you start taking lessons, and I am sorry to tell you I can't answer that. I think that's something that your family can decide. Maybe your parents can talk about your interest in music with some piano teachers in your area. Until you take lessons, though, you can find many ways to enjoy the piano. When I was a boy, I liked to make music for whatever I was feeling. I started playing the piano when I was five years old. I'd make up songs that were happy or sad or angry or

silly. Music and feelings can go together in so many ways. I'm glad to know you're interested in music, too, Gregory, and I hope that you'll find many ways to enjoy music your whole life long.

Dear Mister Rogers,
Locally, we are holding a regional symposium . . . to
address the question, "What is most worth knowing?"
. . . You can help a lot of youngsters . . . by responding.
                    The Oregon School Administrators

Dear Neighbors,
What I believe is most worth knowing is that every human being has value. This is the basis of all healthy relationships; and it's through relationships that we grow and learn best.

I've learned what is most worth knowing through living each day as it is given to me. It cannot be "taught" but it can be "caught" from those who live their lives right along with us. What a privilege to be able to look for the good in our "neighbor"!

Dear Mister Rogers,
Now that I'm grown-up (26), I will be getting married
soon for the first time. What's the best piece of advice
you could give me?

Karen

Dear Karen,

. . . It was exciting to know about your upcoming
marriage, and I send our very best wishes to you and
to your fiancé.

I was touched to know you wanted some of my
thoughts about marriage, and I thought you might like
to have the enclosed copy of a page from our book
Mister Rogers Talks with Parents. . . . Everyone in our
Neighborhood wishes you and your future husband a
lifetime of caring and a lifetime of growing.

❀ Here is an excerpt from the page we sent to Karen:

"Love" is a word to use with care. It means many
different things and can be expressed in many different
ways. But I think it means that a person can grow to
his or her fullest capacity only in mutually caring
relationships with other human beings.

Mutually caring relationships require kindness and patience, tolerance, optimism, joy in others' achievements, confidence in oneself, and the ability to give without undue thought of gain. We need to accept the fact that it is not in the power of any human being to provide all these things all the time. For any of us, mutually caring relationships will also always include some measure of unkindness and impatience, intolerance, pessimism, envy, self-doubt, and disappointment.

Love doesn't mean a state of perfect caring. To love someone is to strive to accept that person exactly the way he or she is, right here and now—and to go on caring through joyful times and through times that may bring us pain.

Dear Mister Rogers,
. . . What do you consider to be the most important advice that a father could give to his child?

Jeff

Dear Jeff,

It was a delight to share in your anticipation of being a father some day, and I'm glad to know that you look forward to using what we offer to support you in your important work of fathering. You asked for some advice, and I thought the best way to offer that is through some of our writings.

You've certainly made this a bright day for all of us here in the Neighborhood, and we send our very best wishes for all that is ahead for you. You are special!

❀ Here are some of the ideas in the writings we sent to Jeff:

Parenthood is not learned: Parenthood is an inner change. Being a parent is a complex thing. It involves not only trying to feel what our children are feeling, but also trying to understand our own needs and feelings that our children evoke. That's why I have always said that parenthood gives us another chance to grow.

There is one universal need that we all share: We all long to be cared for, and that longing lies at the root of our ability to care for our children. If the day ever came when we were able to accept ourselves and our children exactly as we and they are, then I believe we would have come very close to an ultimate understanding of what "good" parenting means.

It's part of being human to fall short of that total acceptance and that ultimate understanding—and often far short. But the most important gifts a parent can give a child are the gifts of our unconditional love and our respect for that child's uniqueness.

Looking back over the years of parenting that my wife and I have had with our two boys, I feel good about who we are and what we've done. I don't mean we were perfect parents. Not at all. Our years with our children were marked by plenty of inappropriate responses. Both Joanne and I can recall many times when we wish we'd said or done something different. But we didn't, and we've learned not to feel too guilty about that. What gives us our good feelings about our parenting is that we always cared and always tried to do our best.

Dear Mister Rogers,

We are doing a project in language class to see if writing is important in the real world. There are a few questions I want to ask about writing. First, how do you use writing in your career? Second, do you think it's important for kids to learn how to write well and have good writing habits? Do you feel writing is as hard for you as it is for us?

Josh, eighth-grader

Dear Josh,

It meant a great deal to me that you wanted to write to me as part of your language class project. You are fortunate to have a teacher who is helping you learn about writing in such a personal and interesting way.

Writing is an essential part of my work. I write the scripts for our television programs and the lyrics for the Neighborhood songs I compose. I answer the mail from colleagues and from our viewers. I have written lots of articles and speeches and a number of books for children and for adults.

There's something I've learned about writing that I'd like to pass on to you and the others in your language class. How our words are understood doesn't depend just on how we as writers express our ideas. It also depends on how the other person receives what we're saying. I think the most important part about writing is the *listening* that we do beforehand so that we can get to know the reader. When we can truly respect what that person brings to what we're offering, that's felt by the reader and makes the written communication all the more meaningful.

You also wanted to know if I think it is important for students to learn to write well. YES! It isn't easy to communicate our thoughts and feelings in writing, and too often I've seen conflicts and problems come from misinterpreting what someone has written. Being able to write well takes a lot of hard work—and a lot of patience through revision after revision. It also takes a lot of acceptance of things that aren't perfect and the willingness to believe that "the next thing I write will be even better."

❀ When people ask for advice, I sometimes get the feeling they think only "experts" have the answers. Sometimes it seems that they just want an "expert" to verify that they're on the right track. Even though I applaud reaching out for help, at the same time, I firmly believe the best answers are the ones that feel right to those of us who are living through the questions. I hope that the people who write to our Neighborhood can trust their own intuition about whatever answer comes from me or from any other "professional" they may ask.

Nobody has all the answers. We're all growing in this world together.

CHAPTER TEN

How did you get your face on your face on all our pennies?

(Peter, age 6)

❁ Many days the mail brings us treasures—letters that cheer us and brighten our whole Neighborhood. They are such fun to read! In this chapter we've included some of them for you to enjoy. I hope you'll let them nourish you. I will always feel blessed to be addressed as Dear Mister Rogers.

Dear Mister Rogers,
How did you get on all our pennies?
  Your face is on the front and your Trolley's on the back . . .

Penn, age 4

Dear Mister Rogers,
The world is so wonderful through a child's eyes. A penny is a trolley and a half-eaten piece of bread is an imaginary friend.

Peter, Miriam's dad

Dear Mister Rogers,
Erika used to think the word for television was "Mister Rogers" since you were the only program she had seen on TV!

Hannah, Erika's mom

Dear Mister Rogers,
Maddy is 2 years old, and loves Bob Dog. She calls you "Mick Ja-Ja." We think she has you mixed up with one of the Rolling Stones!

Sarah, Maddy's mom

Dear Mister Rogers,
My son, Mikey . . . although a major fan, does not have a clear mental picture of you. The night before the presidential election when Michael Dukakis [presidential candidate, then governor of Massachusetts] appeared on television wearing a casual sweater and loafers, Mikey started proclaiming, "It's Mister Rogers . . . Mister Rogers." Mikey seemed a little distraught and confused when you—in the guise of Michael Dukakis— started rambling on about defense spending and furlough programs.

Robert, Mikey's dad

Dear MisDr Rojrs,
I Trid Yor ResoP Ov Sbgete. Hppy Valntis Day.
        Sarah, age 6

Dear Mister Rogers,
Please come for dinner. I will cook. Thank you.
        Amanda, age 4

Dear Mister Rogers,
On our way [to the museum] yesterday, Emily (age 4
and a half) was asking many questions concerning this
place she was about to see. She kept asking if the rooms
were round, and I just answered that it was a big square
building, without questioning why she had such a "silly"
notion about the shape of the rooms. . . . It wasn't until
we were home later that evening, that I discovered why
Emily had all those questions about the museum having
round rooms. We were . . . telling her father about our
day, when she brought up the shape of the rooms again.
It then occurred to me that she was using her only prior
image of a museum, the Museum-Go-Round from the
Neighborhood of Make-Believe, as her reference.
        Darlene, Emily's mom

Dear Mister Rogers,
When Daniel was two and a half, and we were waiting
for our new baby to be born, we once asked Dan about
what name he would like for the new baby. "Mister
Rogers" was his answer.

Mary, Daniel's mom

Dear Mister Rogers,
Elizabeth (5 years old) was angry a few months ago and
started to kick at one of the cupboard doors. I said,
"Elizabeth, that is not appropriate. If you're angry, go
pound a pillow." She looked at me and without missing
a beat said, "Oh, Mom, you've been watching too much
Mister Rogers!" We all cracked up, and the anger was
gone.

Jim and Jan, Elizabeth's parents

Dear Mister Rogers,
If you are the Fred Rogers my little sister watches every
day then, "Hi!" When I was little you used to be my
favorite T.V. show host. . . . Oh, I'm sorry but I cannot
be your neighbor (I live in Alaska).

Sy, age 11

Dear Mister Rogers,
In your younger years did you get a lot of chicks because
you were Mister Rogers?

Tyler, age 17

Dear Mister Rogers,
I think you should be the president, but you should still
be on tv Saturday.

Amanda, age 5

Dear Mister Rogers,
I like your television visits. I would like to say to you it
is nice to have televisions. I am Erik—4½, and I know
one plus one equals two. . . . When I watch your show
everything is neat. I like the Make-Believe. I forgot what
else to say.

Erik, age 4½

Dear Erik,
. . . You'll remember next time.
Your Television Friend,

Mister Rogers

FOR THE BEST IN PAPERBACKS, LOOK FOR THE

In every corner of the world, on every subject under the sun, Penguin represents quality and variety—the very best in publishing today.

For complete information about books available from Penguin—including Puffins, Penguin Classics, and Arkana—and how to order them, write to us at the appropriate address below. Please note that for copyright reasons the selection of books varies from country to country.

In the United Kingdom: Please write to *Dept. JC, Penguin Books Ltd, FREEPOST, West Drayton, Middlesex UB7 0BR.*

If you have any difficulty in obtaining a title, please send your order with the correct money, plus ten percent for postage and packaging, to *P.O. Box No. 11, West Drayton, Middlesex UB7 0BR*

In the United States: Please write to *Consumer Sales, Penguin USA, P.O. Box 999, Dept. 17109, Bergenfield, New Jersey 07621-0120.* VISA and MasterCard holders call 1-800-253-6476 to order all Penguin titles

In Canada: Please write to *Penguin Books Canada Ltd, 10 Alcorn Avenue, Suite 300, Toronto, Ontario M4V 3B2*

In Australia: Please write to *Penguin Books Australia Ltd, P.O. Box 257, Ringwood, Victoria 3134*

In New Zealand: Please write to *Penguin Books (NZ) Ltd, Private Bag 102902, North Shore Mail Centre, Auckland 10*

In India: Please write to *Penguin Books India Pvt Ltd, 706 Eros Apartments, 56 Nehru Place, New Delhi 110 019*

In the Netherlands: Please write to *Penguin Books Netherlands bv, Postbus 3507, NL-1001 AH Amsterdam*

In Germany: Please write to *Penguin Books Deutschland GmbH, Metzlerstrasse 26, 60594 Frankfurt am Main*

In Spain: Please write to *Penguin Books S.A., Bravo Murillo 19, 1° B, 28015 Madrid*

In Italy: Please write to *Penguin Italia s.r.l., Via Felice Casati 20, I-20124 Milano*

In France: Please write to *Penguin France S.A., 17 rue Lejeune, F-31000 Toulouse*

In Japan: Please write to *Penguin Books Japan, Ishikiribashi Building, 2-5-4, Suido, Bunkyo-ku, Tokyo 112*

In Greece: Please write to *Penguin Hellas Ltd, Dimocritou 3, GR-106 71 Athens*

In South Africa: Please write to *Longman Penguin Southern Africa (Pty) Ltd, Private Bag X08, Bertsham 2013*